Corpus-Based Studies on Non-Finite Complements in Recent English

Paul Rickman • Juhani Rudanko

Corpus-Based Studies on Non-Finite Complements in Recent English

palgrave
macmillan

Paul Rickman
English Language,
Literature and Translation
University of Tampere
Tampere, Finland

Juhani Rudanko
English Language,
Literature and Translation
University of Tampere
Tampere, Finland

ISBN 978-3-319-72988-6   ISBN 978-3-319-72989-3   (eBook)
https://doi.org/10.1007/978-3-319-72989-3

Library of Congress Control Number: 2018930498

Cover illustration: Détail de la Tour Eiffel © nemesis2207/Fotolia.co.uk

Printed on acid-free paper

This Palgrave Pivot imprint is published by Springer Nature
The registered company is Springer International Publishing AG
The registered company address is: Gewerbestrasse 11, 6330 Cham, Switzerland

ACKNOWLEDGMENTS

It is our pleasure to thank Palgrave Macmillan for accepting this book for publication in the Palgrave Pivot series, and the editors and assistants who have helped us during the process.

In this work we have included sections of a paper that was written by both authors, and originally published by John Benjamins: Chapter 5 appeared in 2014 in Kristin Davidse, Caroline Gentens, Lobke Ghesquière & Lieven Vandelanotte, eds., *Corpus Interrogation and Grammatical Patterns*, 209–221, Amsterdam/Philadelphia: John Benjamins. We are grateful to John Benjamins for granting permission for the work to be republished here.

This work has benefitted from the comments of two anonymous readers, and it is to them that the current authors express gratitude. Some of the chapters in this book have been presented at various conferences over the past few years, and the suggestions arising from those sessions have similarly helped add new dimensions to our work. Special thanks must also go to Professor Mark Davies and his assistants at Brigham Young University, whose freely available family of corpora have supplied the data that have enabled us to carry out this research. It is quite likely that without it, this book would not have been written. We are, of course, solely responsible for the use we have made of the corpora, and for any remaining errors and inadequacies in the book.

CONTENTS

LIST OF FIGURES

LIST OF TABLES

CHAPTER 1

Introduction

Abstract This chapter introduces the central theoretical concerns taken up in the subsequent chapters, laying the necessary groundwork for the discussions of subject and object control, and provides a preview of the content and aims of the rest of the book. Key issues include the postulation of understood arguments in non-finite complements, and the status of *to* as both an infinitive marker and a preposition. The continuation of work on the Choice Principle in the context of adjectival complementation is a major theme in the book, and a brief introduction to the Principle is also provided here. Motivation for the present work is given, as well as a discussion of the corpora used to provide the data.

Keywords Subject control • Object control • Choice Principle • Great Complement Shift • Bach's Generalization

It must be acknowledged at the outset that the type of work presented here owes a large debt to the creation (and the creators) and widespread availability of the large electronic corpora of today. Studies of the type presented in this volume would, to some extent, have been possible enough without them, but it goes without saying that the process leading to publication would have been far more exhausting, and the publication itself undoubtedly less exhaustive. The corpora we have relied on here include a selection from the family compiled and/or made available by

© The Author(s) 2018
P. Rickman, J. Rudanko, *Corpus-Based Studies on Non-Finite Complements in Recent English*,
https://doi.org/10.1007/978-3-319-72989-3_1

Mark Davies at Brigham Young University—the Corpus of Contemporary American English, the Corpus of Historical American English, Hansard—in addition to the well-known British National Corpus. A general aim of all of the upcoming chapters is the study of regional variation and diachronic change pertaining to aspects of the sentential complementation system of selected English predicates, both adjectival and verbal. A diachronic perspective is a feature of all four studies, and in some cases the target patterns are not overly abundant in earlier time periods of English, which makes the contribution of two of the aforementioned corpora indispensable due to their collective provision of well over two billion words covering the past two centuries of English.

The issue of control is at the heart of all the work presented in the forthcoming chapters—Chapters 2, 3, and 4 deal with subject control in adjectival predicate constructions with *scared, terrified* and *afraid,* while object control with the verbal predicate *warn* is the focus of Chap. 5. To begin, we establish the theoretical framework on matters related to control in general, and to this end, it will be useful to consider examples (1a–b), taken from COCA, the Corpus of Contemporary American English:

(1)   a.   …Santa, do you intend to wear that outfit in July in Chicago?   (1997, SPOK)
      b.   Only eight male participants admitted to wearing a toupee.   (1994, MAG)

Examples (1a–b) illustrate subject control with the verbal predicates *intend* and *admit. Intend* is a predicate that, among other possibilities, can govern a *to* infinitive clause, as it does in (1a). *Admit,* in (1b), meanwhile, takes an *-ing* clause preceded by *to,* although with *admit* the *-ing* clause is also commonly found without *to.* It should be made clear here that, given that the present work is concerned with control, it is necessary to disregard the other, non-relevant complements that are also commonly selected by the matrix verbs in question. These include both NP and finite sentential complements, neither of which has the properties needed to invoke a discussion of control.

Each of the examples in (1a–b) comprises two sentences or clauses. A common assumption made in much of the work carried out in this area is that in such structures there exists an unrealized element—the null subject of the lower clause verb, which, in both cases, is *wear.* This understood subject is typically given the label PRO. The postulation of understood elements in such structures is not something that is universally accepted, but nonetheless has been a major feature of much influential work in this area throughout the past several decades. The idea is found in much of the early literature, before the coining of the term PRO, but the basic idea is nonetheless the same (Kajita 1967; Rosenbaum 1967). It is also found in later work (Chomsky 1986, 114–131; Culicover 1997, 75–85; Davies and Dubinsky 2004), where it is often noted that the presence of PRO makes it possible to maintain the Theta Criterion, which states that "[e]ach argument bears one and only one Θ-role, and each Θ-role is assigned to one and only one argument" (Chomsky 1981, 36).[1] Further, the postulation of an understood subject is also presented as an accepted and uncontroversial view in mainstream, influential grammars of English in recent times, as this excerpt from Huddleston and Pullum (2002, 65) shows: "[m]ost non-finite clauses have no overt subject, but the interpretation of the clause requires that an understood subject be retrieved from the linguistic or non-linguistic context" (see also Brinton and Brinton 2010, 275). This view is adopted in the present work.

The reference to retrieving an understood subject "from the linguistic or non-linguistic context" points to the notion of control:

> Control has to do primarily with the question of what determines the identity of the unexpressed subject of non-finite verbal forms such as the infinitive or the gerund-participle in constructions such as *Joseph tried to find a quiet place* and *Peter enjoyed going fishing in his boat*. (Duffley 2014, 13)[2]

The present authors view control as an interpretive notion that is not strictly syntactic (see the quote from Huddleston and Pullum 2002 above).[3] It is nevertheless the case that it is helpful to distinguish two main types of control, subject control and object control. In the case of subject control structures, as in (1a–b), PRO is coreferential with the subject of the matrix clause, *you* in (1a), and *eight male participants* in (1b). Sentences (1a–b) are rewritten below—and abbreviated where appropriate—to show the level of sentence structure necessary to bring out the understood argument.

(1)   a′.   [[you]$_{NP}$ [intend]$_{Verb1}$ [[PRO]$_{NP}$ [to]$_{Infl}$ [[wear]$_{Verb2}$ that outfit]$_{VP}$]$_{S2}$]$_{S1}$

       b′.   [[Only eight male participants]$_{NP}$ [admitted]$_{Verb1}$ [to]$_{PREP}$ [[[PRO]$_{NP}$ [[wearing]$_{Verb2}$ a toupee]$_{VP}$]$_{S2}$]$_{NP}$]$_{S1}$

Another important theoretical issue concerns the status and position of the word *to* in (1a–b). *To* is labeled infl in (1a′) and appears after PRO, and prep in (1b′), appearing before PRO. Thus, in the former, *to* is seen as an infinitival marker, and placed under the Infl (or Aux) node, whereas its function in (1b′) is that of preposition. Again, this is a view that is not without its critics, but in the mainstream opinion, *to* does indeed perform separate functions (Bybee 2003, 159; Haspelmath 1989; Quirk et al. 1985, 1178f), and is held to do so also in the present work.[4]

As for the infinitive and the -*ing* lower clauses themselves, while they do share some common properties, they are dissimilar in one important respect. This can be highlighted by demonstrating that each responds differently to various standard tests involving movement and substitution, as in (2a–d) (for a substitution test, see also Duffley 2000, 231).

(2)   a.   What did eight male participants admit to? Wearing a toupee.
      b.   *What does Santa intend to? Wear that outfit in July.
      c.   What eight male participants admitted to was wearing a toupee
      d.   *What Santa intends to is wear that outfit in July.

The transformations in (2a–b) and (2c–d), *wh* question formation and pseudo clefting respectively, bring to light the important point that the -*ing* clause, or gerund in this case, in the *to* -*ing* pattern is a nominal clause—a sentence dominated by an NP. No such claim can be made for the *to* infinitive on the other hand, which cannot be questioned in a *wh* question or placed in the focal position in a pseudo cleft structure without the required *do* support.

The other type of control dealt with here is object control. Consider (3a–b), both of which are taken from COCA.

(3)   a.   ...the carpenter told Jack to go to the shop for nails.   (2015, FIC)
      b.   The police chief accused Bridges of neglecting his unpaid duties   (2014,
           as mayor...   NEWS)

The discussion of PRO above also applies to object control, where in this case the understood subjects of *go* in (3a) and *neglect* in (3b) are coreferential with the matrix clause objects, the NPs *Jack* and *Bridges* respectively. The lower clause in (3a), a *to* infinitive, is a complement commonly selected by *tell*, and the lower clause in (3b) is an -*ing* clause preceded by the preposition *of*; the complement here is termed an *of* -*ing* complement, a common selection for verbs of the *accuse* type. The arguments given above, in connection with the status of the infinitive marker *to*, and the differences between the *to* infinitive and the *-ing* clause, also apply here, and need not be repeated.

In the four chapters that follow, three subject control predicates and one object control predicate are examined in detail. For subject control, we further test a recently proposed principle that has been proven to shed light on the distributional tendencies of competing complement types in adjectival subject control structures. The adjectival predicates share a common feature in their ability to select the same key non-finite complements, such that the non-finite complements in question are sufficiently similar in their uses to be considered constructional competitors. In the case of the object control chapter, the investigation concerns a class of exceptions to a general principle concerning the omission of an element of the argument structure in these types of patterns. The class of exceptions involves an emerging gerundial pattern that can likewise be viewed as a constructional competitor of a more "regular" gerundial pattern. A major concern of the present study is to examine the nature of such constructional competition affecting the distribution of the complementation patterns in question in recent English. This entails a partly diachronic perspective. Such a perspective is fairly new in work on complementation, as has been noted for instance by D'hoedt and Cuyckens (2017). They write:

> It is only in the last twenty years or so that diachronic studies have appeared which present broad accounts of change and variation in complementation patterns in different periods of the history of English (see Fischer 1995; Fanego 1996a, 1996b, 1998; Rudanko 1998, 2006, 2010, 2012; Miller 2002; Los 2005; Rohdenburg 2006; De Smet 2008, 2013), attesting to a distributional reorganization of CCs [complement clauses] over time. [Note omitted] (D'hoedt and Cuyckens 2017, 118)

The present study with its focus on selected types of control constructions and their evolution is offered as a contribution to this new and emerging area of research. As noted above, the data for all forthcoming chapters is sourced from some of the world's largest corpora of American and British English.

Turning to the more specific consideration of individual chapters, Chap. 2 is the first of three related studies into subject control with adjectival predicates denoting states of fear. The adjective *scared* is examined here, with data on American English, from COHA going back as far as the 1820s, and on British English, from the BNC. The relevant rival complements are the *to* infinitive and the *of -ing* patterns, as illustrated in (4a–b).

(4) a. "It's a bother you can't swim. Will you be scared to get in   (COHA, 1932,
with me?"   FIC)
b. ...he was scared of getting that knife in his back.   (COHA, 2000,
FIC)

It can be said that the two types of complement illustrated in (4a–b) are very similar in meaning, and it would be reasonable to assume that some speakers might use the *to* infinitive and the *of -ing* complements interchangeably in many contexts, particularly with the same lower verb. The similarity in meaning and use between the two constructions poses a challenge for the assumption that "a difference in syntactic form always spells a difference in meaning" (Bolinger 1968, 127). This well-established hypothesis has been called Bolinger's Generalization, and it provides a guiding rule of thumb in the series of studies in this book. In the spirit of the principle we probe the semantic boundary that exists between the complements illustrated in (4a–b). A recently developed theory that may afford some insight into complement distribution in such cases has been termed the Choice Principle (Rudanko 2010). It is based upon consideration of the semantic role of the understood subject of the lower clause. The role of the understood subject of the lower verb *get in* in (4a), for example, can be seen as that of Agent, and as such, its referent has a choice as regards the performance or non-performance of the action described by the lower verb; (4a) is thus a typical example of a [+Choice] context. The subject of *get* in (4b), on the other hand, is more in line with the role of Patient; in this case there is clearly less choice on the part of the referent of the subject in relation to the performance of the lower verb action. The lower predicate of (4b) is therefore an example of a [−Choice] environment. The Choice Principle predicts that the *to* infinitive complement is more conducive to a [+Choice] context, while the *of -ing* type tends to be more readily linked to the [−Choice] context. The American English data of the last three decades of the twentieth century are compared to the data taken from the BNC, and the relative complement selection tendencies in the two varieties are discussed.

Chapter 3 builds on the work of Chap. 2 in a continuation of the study of the *fear*-type adjectives against the backdrop of the Choice Principle, with the previously lesser-studied adjective *terrified*. Data is collected from COHA, and, due to the relative paucity of data on this particular adjective, the historical COHA data is supplemented with data from COCA to provide a more comprehensive appraisal of the situation in recent English. As in Chap. 2, data from the BNC is introduced and comparisons are drawn between the two varieties. As noted above, and shown by (5a–b), *terrified* is capable of selecting the same two complement types as *scared*.

(5) a. They were terrified to go out into the heart of the Bronx   (COHA, 1987,
          at noon...   FIC)
     b. At first she was terrified of going back to school.   (COHA, 1993,
                                                                       MAG)

As was the case with *scared*, it is investigated whether the Choice Principle is also applicable to the lower clause environments of the adjective *terrified*, that is, whether *to* infinitives show a connection to the [+Choice] type of lower clause, and whether the *of-ing* complement couples most naturally with the [−Choice] lower clause type. The examples shown in (5a–b), however, are both indexed as [+Choice], and the semantic difference between them is more subtle than that seen in a clear [+Choice] and [−Choice] contrast, as was seen in examples (4a–b). The semantic boundary between the two constructions may thus be unclear, and meanings may be difficult to tease apart. We explore the possible explanations and attempt to delimit them on the basis of agentivity and control over the action predicated by the lower verb.

Chapter 4 completes the survey of *fear* adjectives, with the predicate *afraid*. This is by far the most frequently used of the adjectives examined in this series overall, and its occurrence with the two target complements is sufficiently frequent to provide a large dataset. For this reason only three evenly spaced decades from COHA were sourced for data: the 1820s, the 1910s, and the 2000s. In the spirit of the previous two chapters, the BNC provides data enabling a comparison of the present-day situation in British English and American English. Examples (6a–b) provide illustrations.

(6) a. The high, excited voice raved on: "I'm afraid to die! I'm   (COHA, 1917,
          afraid of that Presence!"   FIC)
     b. I'm just as afraid of having Farmer Weeks catch us as you are. (COHA, 1914,
                                                                       FIC)

These examples both exemplify [−Choice] lower clause environments, and, alongside (5a–b), they serve to illustrate the point, made in earlier work (Rudanko 2017, 54), that the Choice Principle, like most other principles and generalizations, linguistic and otherwise, cannot be seen as a categorical rule without exceptions. The task of the researcher then is to apply the Choice Principle to fresh data and previously uncharted areas with the aim of further illuminating the degree of certainty that can be expected from such a tool. The measures of statistical significance that are provided in all cases concerning the Choice Principle in this book are therefore vital, and act as methodological footholds for the next step in the exploratory process.

While the application of the Choice Principle to these previously under-explored cases of complement variation is the main goal of these first three studies, this type of infinitival-gerundial competition lends itself readily to the application of another generalization, already well-established in the literature, which has been shown to shed light on complement distributional tendencies. The Extraction Principle (Vosberg 2003a, b), a syntactic rather than semantic factor, predicts that in environments showing the extraction of clausal elements for the purposes of relativization, question formation and so on, the infinitival complement will be the more likely choice of the two competing types. All data is filtered first through the non-semantic lens of the Extraction Principle, and given that the Principle has been shown to have a significant effect on complement selection, all tokens evidencing extraction are then set aside before we consider the remaining data in the semantic light of the Choice Principle.

In addition, all data must be viewed against the overall backdrop of the Great Complement Shift (Rohdenburg 2006, 2014; Vosberg 2006, 2009; Rudanko 2010, 2011, 2012, 2015, 2017; Fanego 2016). This term designates a range of related generalizations about a set of grammatical changes discovered and brought together in an effort to provide a model of the general dynamics of the system of English complementation patterns in recent centuries. One key aspect of this concerns the overall increase in the use of gerundial complements in recent English, an increase that has often come at the cost of the earlier established infinitival option (see also Fanego 1996a, 1996b, 2007; Rudanko 2006; Leech et al. 2009, 185–186). It can be stated already at this point that we take it as given that the effects of the Shift will be evident to some degree in the upcoming analyses of the adjectival predicates in Chaps. 2, 3 and 4. It is the actual extent to which the gerund has infiltrated the infinitival territory of each predicate and the process of change involved that we hope to be able to provide some more information on with this work.

Chapter 5 moves on to object control with the verbal predicate *warn*. The aim is to expand upon earlier work done on *warn* in American English (Rudanko and Rickman 2014) by incorporating British English data from Hansard, thus providing a comparison between the two main varieties. Consider examples (7a–b).

(7) a. However, I warn the hon: Gentleman against using phrases such as   (Hansard,
          "out of control"...   2003)
     b. However, I warn against putting them in the straitjacket of a   (Hansard,
          written constitution...   1994)

This chapter focuses on the issue of the omitted object in object control structures, as exemplified in (7b). It can be seen that the object of *warn* in (7b)—designating the person (or persons) receiving the warning—is not specified overtly. Such structures can be seen as violations of what has been called Bach's Generalization (Bach 1980, 304; Bresnan 1982, 418–419; Rizzi 1986), which states that the matrix clause object must be expressed overtly in object control structures. In (7a) this is the case, and the recipient of the warning is explicitly spelled out.

In Rudanko and Rickman (2014) it was found that in American English the covert object construction increased in frequency over the course of the twentieth century, and a concomitant decrease in frequency was evident in the overt object construction. The verb *warn* might therefore be said to be undergoing a detransitivization process, no longer requiring a direct object to be present in certain contexts. The objective here is to shed further light on this finding and to expand upon it by introducing diachronic data from British English. One of the hypotheses put forward in the previous work done on *warn* was that the covert object option with this verb might be particularly convenient to those who are required to employ some diplomacy in issuing warnings, namely politicians. The Hansard corpus is thus suited to the task, being large, diachronic, and, most importantly, of the appropriate text type.[5] It is suggested that the pragmatic requirement in some registers of English for such a construction with a verb such as *warn* may be a decisive factor in the detransitivization process that *warn* appears to be undergoing.

Finally, we offer a comment on an important methodological issue concerning the primary mode of research underpinning the work contained in this book, not to mention some of the earlier work of both authors. This approach is one of the two outlined in this passage from Leech et al. (2009, 181):

> If we decide to focus on a specific non-finite complement structure—such as, say, the *to*-infinitive clause or the gerund with possessive/genitive modifier—we will find these structures serving a large variety of functions, with most of them not being involved in current diachronic change. If, on the other hand, we decide to focus on more specific constructions—combinations of particular superordinate predicates and particular patterns of complementation (such as, for example, variation between infinitives and gerunds with *accustomed to*)—we can easily home in on areas of ongoing diachronic change, without, however, being able to correlate individual shifts in usage preferences with general trends in the evolution of the system of English non-finite verbal forms.

With a primary focus on the "more specific constructions," the second of the two approaches described above and the approach adopted by the present authors, there is indeed the potential risk that the researcher may fail to link the details of a particular matrix predicate with wider trends, and Leech et al. are correct to point out the problem here. The inability to relate the results of detailed investigations into individual matrix predicates to wider trends, though, might be mitigated somewhat by the very large and balanced corpora that are becoming increasingly available today, and even in the case of infrequent constructions, sufficient data can often be gleaned so as to allow the researcher to map individual results onto wider trends.

Despite the problems that may arise when adopting this perspective, the benefits of the attention to detail inherent in this approach should not, however, be underestimated, and with many pieces of the bigger picture of variation and change in the English complement system still missing, it is precisely those details that are needed to provide the missing pieces. It is the evidence that they provide that helps to further refine and validate the larger principles that form the foundation of the entire field of study. The related and complementary studies into control in adjectival and verbal predicate constructions offered in this book were carried out with the intention of contributing to the bigger picture, and refining our perspective on, and our understanding of, the way we use the English language.

Notes

1. Postal (1970) predates the coining of PRO and the full formulation of Binding theory, but his discussion offers important evidence for the need for understood subjects in infinitival and gerundial clauses. For the Binding theory argument for PRO, see also Landau (2013, 75).
2. In Duffley's second example the *-ing* form is a gerund-participle in the terminology that he uses. However, in the present volume the more traditional label "gerund" is used for the *-ing* form in the type of sentence illustrated by Duffley.
3. For a comprehensive study of different approaches to control in generative grammar, see Landau (2013).
4. It has sometimes been argued that infinitival *to* is a "dummy (i.e. meaningless) functor with no intrinsic semantic content" (Radford 1997, 52), but the present authors prefer to think that infinitival *to*, similarly to other constituents under the Infl (or Aux) node, may carry a meaning. (For further comments, see Chap. 2.)
5. Mollin (2007) notes that Hansard transcripts may sometimes suffer from some transcription problems. However, it is not clear that the problems brought to light involve the omission or insertion of a particular type of object. Therefore, pending the compilation of a similarly large diachronic corpus of British English, the investigator seems justified in using the Hansard Corpus as a source of data in this type of study.

References

Bach, Emmon. 1980. In Defense of Passive. *Linguistics and Philosophy* 3: 297–341.

Bolinger, Dwight. 1968. Entailment and the Meaning of Structures. *Glossa* 2: 119–127.

Bresnan, Joan. 1982. Control and Complementation. *Linguistic Inquiry* 13 (3): 343–434.

Brinton, Laurel J., and Donna M. Brinton. 2010. *The Linguistic Structure of Modern English*. Amsterdam and Philadelphia: John Benjamins.

Bybee, Joan. 2003. Cognitive Processes in Grammaticalization. In *The New Psychology of Language*, ed. Michael Tomasello, vol. 2, 145–167. Mahwah, NJ: Lawrence Erlbaum.

Chomsky, Noam. 1981. *Lectures on Government and Binding*. Dordrecht: Foris.

———. 1986. *Knowledge of Language: Its Nature, Origin and Use*. New York: Praeger.

Culicover, Peter. 1997. *Principles and Parameters*. Oxford: Oxford University Press.

Davies, William, and Stanley Dubinsky. 2004. *The Grammar of Raising and Control*. Malden, MA: Blackwell.

De Smet, Hendrik. 2008. *Diffusional Change in the English System of Complementation. Gerunds, Participles and* for…to *Infinitives*. Doctoral Dissertation, Catholic University of Leuven.

———. 2013. *Spreading Patterns. Diffusional Change in the English System of Complementation*. Oxford: Oxford University Press.

D'hoedt, Frauke, and Hubert Cuyckens. 2017. Finite, Infinitival and Verbless Complementation: The Case of *Believe, Suppose* and *Find*. In *Infinitives at the Syntax-Semantics Interface: A Diachronic Perspective*, ed. Lukasz Jedrzejowski and Ulrike Demske, 115–145. Berlin: De Gruyter.

Duffley, Patrick J. 2000. Gerund versus Infinitive as Complement of Transitive Verbs in English: The Problems of 'Tense' and 'Control'. *Journal of English Linguistics* 28: 221–248.

———. 2014. *Reclaiming Control as a Semantic and Pragmatic Phenomenon*. Amsterdam and Philadelphia: John Benjamins.

Fanego, Teresa. 1996a. The Development of Gerunds as Objects of Subject-Control Verbs in English (1400–1760). *Diachronica* 13: 29–62.

———. 1996b. The Gerund in Early Modern English: Evidence from the Helsinki Corpus. *Folia Linguistica Historica* XVII: 97–152.

———. 1998. Developments in Argument Linking in Early Modern English Gerund Phrases. *English Language and Linguistics* 2 (1): 87–119.

———. 2007. Drift and the Development of Sentential Complements in British and American English from 1700 to the Present Day. In *"Of Varying Language and Opposing Creed": New Insights into Late Modern English*, ed. Javier Pérez-Guerra, Dolores González-Álvarez, Jorge L. Bueno-Alonso, and Esperanza Rama-Martínez, 161–235. Linguistic Insights Series 28. Bern, Switzerland: Peter Lang.

———. 2016. The Great Complement Shift Revisited: The Constructionalization of ACC-ing Gerundives. *Functions of Language* 23 (1): 84–119.

Fischer, Olga. 1995. The Distinction between *to* and Bare Infinitival Complements in Late Middle English. *Diachronica* 12 (1): 1–30.

Haspelmath, Martin. 1989. From Purposive to Infinitive—A Universal Path of Grammaticization. *Folia Linguistica Historica* 10 (1–2): 287–310.

Huddleston, Rodney, and Geoffrey Pullum. 2002. *The Cambridge Grammar of the English Language*. Cambridge: Cambridge University Press.

Kajita, Masaru. 1967. *A Generative-Transformational Study of Semi-Auxiliaries in Present-day American English*. Tokyo: Sanseido.

Landau, Idan. 2013. *Control in Generative Grammar: A Research Companion*. Cambridge: Cambridge University Press.

Leech, Geoffrey, Marianne Hundt, Christian Mair, and Nicholas Smith. 2009. *Change in Contemporary English*. Cambridge: Cambridge University Press.

Los, Bettelou. 2005. *The Rise of the To-Infinitive*. Oxford: Oxford University Press.

Miller, Gary. 2002. *Nonfinite Structures in Theory and Change*. Oxford: Oxford University Press.

Mollin, Sandra. 2007. The Hansard Hazard: Gauging the Accuracy of British Parliamentary Transcripts. *Corpora* 2 (2): 187–210.

Postal, Paul. 1970. On Coreferential Complement Subject Deletion. *Linguistic Inquiry* 1: 439–500.

Quirk, Randolph, Sidney Greenbaum, Geoffrey Leech, and Jan Svartvik. 1985. *A Comprehensive Grammar of the English Language*. London: Longman.

Radford, Andrew. 1997. *Syntactic Theory and the Structure of English*. Cambridge: Cambridge University Press.

Rizzi, Luigi. 1986. Null Objects in Italian and the Theory of Pro. *Linguistic Inquiry* 17 (3): 501–557.

Rohdenburg, Günter. 2006. The Role of Functional Constraints in the Evolution of the English Complementation System. In *Syntax, Style and Grammatical Norms*, ed. Christiane Dalton-Puffer, Dieter Kastovsky, and Herbert Schendl, 143–166. Bern: Peter Lang.

———. 2014. On the Changing Status of *that*-Clauses. In *Late Modern English Syntax*, ed. Marianne Hundt, 155–181. Cambridge: Cambridge University Press.

Rosenbaum, Peter. 1967. *The Grammar of English Predicate Complement Constructions*. Cambridge: MIT Press.

Rudanko, Juhani. 1998. *Change and Continuity in the English Language: Studies on Complementation over the Past Three Hundred Years*. Lanham, MD: University Press of America.

———. 2006. Watching English Grammar Change. *English Language and Linguistics* 10 (1): 31–48.

———. 2010. Explaining Grammatical Variation and Change: A Case Study of Complementation in American English over Three Decades. *Journal of English Linguistics* 38: 4–24.

———. 2011. *Changes in Complementation in British and American English: Corpus-based Studies on Non-finite Complements in Recent English*. Basingstoke: Palgrave Macmillan.

———. 2012. Exploring Aspects of the Great Complement Shift, with Evidence from the TIME Corpus and COCA. In *The Oxford Handbook of the History of English*, ed. Terttu Nevalainen and Elizabeth Closs Traugott, 222–232. Oxford: Oxford University Press.

———. 2015. *Linking Form and Meaning: Studies on Selected Control Patterns in Recent English*. Basingstoke: Palgrave Macmillan.

———. 2017. *Infinitives and Gerunds in Recent English: Studies on Non-Finite Complements with Data from Large Corpora*. London: Palgrave Macmillan Springer.

Rudanko, Juhani, and Paul Rickman. 2014. Null Objects and Sentential Complements, with Evidence from the Corpus of Historical American English. In *Corpus Interrogation and Grammatical Patterns*, ed. Kristin Davidse, Caroline Gentens, Lobke Ghesquière, and Lieven Vandelanotte, 209–221. Studies in Corpus Linguistics 63. Amsterdam and Philadelphia: John Benjamins.

Vosberg, Uwe. 2003a. The Role of Extractions and *horror aequi* in the Evolution of -*ing* Complements in Modern English. In *Determinants of Grammatical Variation in English*, ed. Günter Rohdenburg and Britta Mondorf, 305–327. Berlin: Mouton de Gruyter.

———. 2003b. Cognitive Complexity and the Establishment of -*ing* Constructions with Retrospective Verbs in Modern English. In *Insights into Late Modern English*, ed. Marina Dossena and Charles Jones, 197–220. Bern: Peter Lang.

———. 2006. *Die grosse Komplementverschiebung*. Tübingen, Germany: Narr.

———. 2009. Non-finite Complements. In *One Language, Two Grammars?* ed. Günter Rohdenburg and Julia Schlüter, 212–227. Cambridge: Cambridge University Press.

CHAPTER 2

Semantic Roles and Complement Selection: A Case Study of the Adjective *Scared*

Abstract When selected by the adjective *scared*, the *to* infinitive and *of* -*ing* constructions can be fairly similar in meaning, and the present study investigates the use and meaning of each type and variation between the two in the last two centuries. A survey is given of the incidence of each type in each decade of COHA, and followed up with data from the BNC, with comments on the adjective from the point of view of the Great Complement Shift. The study then turns to factors influencing the variation between the two types. Attention is paid to the Extraction Principle as a non-semantic factor, and some earlier work on semantic differences is reviewed, but the focus is on a new semantic principle to differentiate between *to* infinitives and gerunds. This is the Choice Principle. The principle concerns the semantic role of the subject of a sentential complement, and establishes a connection between that subject and the type of complement on the basis of the agentivity of the subject in question. The chapter investigates the applicability of the Choice Principle in the case of the adjective *scared* over several decades of COHA, and the implications of the principle for interpreting *to* infinitives and gerundial complements in Late Modern English.

Keywords Subject control • Choice Principle • COHA • BNC

© The Author(s) 2018
P. Rickman, J. Rudanko, *Corpus-Based Studies on Non-Finite Complements in Recent English,*
https://doi.org/10.1007/978-3-319-72989-3_2

15

2.1   INTRODUCTION

"The most important property of complements in clause structure," to quote Huddleston and Pullum, "is that they require the presence of an appropriate verb that **licenses** them" (Huddleston and Pullum 2002, 219). Of course other predicates besides verbs also license complements, but the statement by Huddleston and Pullum captures the key property of complements. It is the purpose of this study to investigate the licensing properties of the adjective *scared*, which is of interest because it licenses more than one type of complement. To illustrate the types to be examined here, consider the examples of usage in (1a–b), from COHA, the Corpus of Historical American English:

(1)   a.   The coolies are scared to come down here.   (1962, FIC)
         b.   … a man who is scared of looking at a fireball.   (1980, FIC)

In both (1a) and (1b) the matrix predicate is the adjective *scared*, and in both it selects a sentential complement. In (1a) the complement is a *to* infinitive clause, and in (1b) it is what is here termed an *of -ing* complement. An assumption adopted here is that in each case the lower clause has its own understood or implicit subject. There are linguists who do not accept the idea of understood subjects, but it formed part of the approach of major traditional grammarians, including Otto Jespersen ([1940] 1961), and understood subjects in non-finite sentences are generally taken for granted in mainstream linguistics today, including Chomsky (1986, 114, 131). As noted in Chap. 1, one reason for this assumption is that understood subjects make it possible to represent the argument structure of the lower verb in a straightforward fashion.

In both (1a) and (1b), the adjective *scared* in the higher clause assigns a theta role to its subject, and as a consequence the understood subject in the lower clause may be represented with the symbol PRO, an "abstract pronominal element" (Chomsky 1981, 6; see also Chomsky 1986, 114–141). In other words, (1a–b) share the property of being control structures. In each case the lower subject is controlled by the higher subject, and both sentences are therefore subject control constructions. The structures of the sentences in (1a–b) may be represented as in (1a′) and (1b′) in their relevant respects.

(1)   a′.   [The coolies are [[scared]$_{Adj}$ [[PRO]$_{NP}$ [to]$_{Aux}$ [come down here]$_{VP}$]$_{S2}$]$_{AdjP}$]$_{S1}$
         b′.   A man [who is [[scared]$_{Adj}$ [[of]$_{Prep}$ [[[PRO]$_{NP}$ looking at a fireball]$_{S2}$]$_{NP}$]$_{PP}$]$_{AdjP}$]$_{S1}$

Structure (1b′) incorporates the traditional notion of a nominal clause, which is represented as a sentence dominated by an NP. The *of* of the *of*-*ing* pattern is of course a preposition and the notion of a nominal clause makes it possible to analyze the PP as consisting of a preposition and an NP dominating a sentence. As for structure (1a′), it incorporates the assumption that the *to* of *to* infinitives is under the Aux node. One consideration in support of the hypothesis that infinitival *to* is under the Aux node in front of a VP in (1a) is that VP Deletion is possible with the adjective *scared* as in (2a), but it is of course not possible in the case of the prepositional *of*-*ing* pattern, as in (2b), where what follows *of* is not a VP. (For the VP Deletion argument, see Radford 1997, 53.)

(2)   a.   I was scared to look at my work, but Max was not scared to.
       b.   *He was scared of looking at a fireball but I was not scared of.

The syntactic structures of (1a–b) are very different, but it is easy to find the two constructions listed side by side as complements of the adjective *scared* in major dictionaries, without being differentiated from the point of view of their meanings. This is the case, for instance, in the seventh edition of the *Oxford Advanced Learner's Dictionary* (*OALD*) (2005), which provides four different constructions— ~ (**of sb/sth**) | ~ (**of doing sth**) | ~ (**to do sth**) | ~ (**that …**)—under the gloss "frightened of sth and afraid that sth bad might happen." The nonsentential *of* NP pattern, while worth noting, is not the primary focus here, and as regards sentential complements of the adjective *scared*, *that* clauses are also set aside here, because they are finite. The present treatment thus only deals with the *to* infinitive and *of*-*ing* patterns among the four. With respect to the two non-finite sentential patterns, the analysis of the adjective in the *OALD* suggests that the two non-finite constructions are close enough to each other to be investigated together and to be compared with each other from the point of view of their use. The purpose of this study is to carry out such a comparison, taking data from recent English into account. A first goal of the comparison is to provide information on the incidence of the two patterns in recent English. A second objective is to consider the potential influence of the Extraction Principle on complement selection in the case of the adjective *scared*. This principle may be formulated as follows:

> In the case of infinitival or gerundial complement options, the infinitive will tend to be favoured in environments where a complement of the subordinate clause is extracted (by topicalization, relativization, comparativization, or interrogation etc.) from its original position and crosses clause boundaries. (Vosberg 2003, 308)

Another objective, and indeed the main objective of this study, is to investigate the nature of the two patterns from the point of view of their meanings. The fact that the two non-finite sentential patterns are found under the same gloss in the *OALD* suggests that they are close to each other in meaning. At the same time, while the two patterns involve control, they represent two different syntactic constructions, and the task of defining and separating the meanings of different constructions is an important area of investigation both in cognitive grammar and in construction grammar. The underlying assumption guiding such work is what is often called Bolinger's Generalization. This says that a "difference in syntactic form always spells a difference in meaning" (Bolinger 1968, 127). The task of separating *to* infinitives from gerunds with respect to their meanings is complex, and a great deal has been written on it. The approach here is based on the novel perspective of the potential influence of the semantic role of the understood subject, assigned by the lower predicate.

The main sources of data are COHA and the BNC. The reason for these choices is that the former is a large and balanced corpus of American English containing more than one text type that covers the last two centuries. The latter was selected as a point of comparison for the last quarter of the twentieth century between British and American English, and, while perhaps not strictly speaking on a par with COHA in terms of text type, it is nonetheless a suitably large and genre-balanced corpus.

2.2   *To* Infinitive and *of*-*ing* Complements of the Adjective *Scared* in COHA

COHA permits tag based searches, and while tags may contain occasional errors, such searches are suitable for identifying historical trends. In the present case, the basic search string for *to* infinitives was "scared to [vʔi*]," where the last term designates the infinitival form of a verb. As regards the *of*-*ing* pattern, the basic search string was "scared of [vʔg*]," where the last term designates the *-ing* form of a verb. The basic search strings were then supplemented with additional search strings allowing the insertion of one or two words between *scared* and *to/of* and search strings allowing the insertion of one word between *to* and the infinitive and between *of* and the gerund.[1]

The search strings for *to* infinitives retrieve a number of tokens of the type of the sentences in (3a–b).

(3)   a.   ... he's too scared to make the break.   (1911, FIC)
        b.   I was too scared to answer, ...   (2001, MAG)

The sentences in (3a–b) have *to* infinitive complements, but in them the *to* infinitive may be what Huddleston and Pullum (2002, 547; see also Quirk et al. 1985, 1140–1142) term an indirect complement, connected to, and licensed by, the modifier *too* in front of the adjective. Such indirect complements are excluded from consideration here.

With indirect complements excluded, the investigation of COHA shows that *to* infinitives have been considerably more frequent than *of -ing* complements with *scared* in the last two centuries. Table 2.1 gives information on the incidence of the two types of complements in the individual decades of COHA. (The normalized frequencies, calculated per million words, are given in parentheses. Basic search strings and additional search strings have been taken into account.). Figure 2.1 depicts the same information in graphic form.

Illustrations of the two types of complements are given in (4a–b) and (5a–b).

(4)   a.   I feel scared to look at that house, ...   (1825, FIC)
        b.   I was scared to ask how it felt.   (1994, FIC)
(5)   a.   I'm scared of skiing down.   (1936, FIC)
        b.   I'm scared of being in the ring with you.   (2001, FIC)

The figures in Table 2.1 show that both *to* infinitive and *of -ing* complements were very rare with the adjective *scared* in the nineteenth century. The complements that were found were of the *to* infinitive type, except for one solitary example of an *of -ing* complement in the 1890s. The table also shows a remarkable rise in the frequency of both patterns in the twentieth century, with *to* infinitives continuing to be more frequent than *of -ing* complements in each decade, and for most decades *to* infinitives are clearly

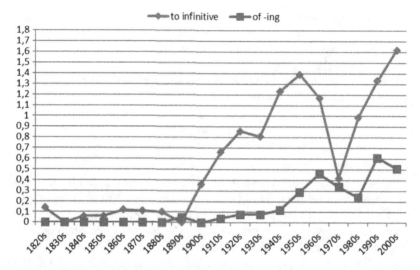

Fig. 2.1 The incidence of *to* infinitive and *of -ing* complements with *scared* in COHA

Table 2.1 *To* infinitive and *of -ing* complements of the adjective *scared* in the decades of COHA

Decade	Size	to infinitives	of -ing complements
1820s	6.9	1 (0.14)	
1830s			
1840s	16.0	1 (0.06)	
1850s	16.5	1 (0.06)	
1860s	17.1	2 (0.12)	
1870s	18.6	2 (0.11)	
1880s	20.3	2 (0.10)	
1890s	20.6		1 (0.05)
1900s	22.1	8 (0.36)	
1910s	22.7	15 (0.66)	1 (0.04)
1920s	25.7	22 (0.86)	2 (0.08)
1930s	24.6	20 (0.81)	2 (0.08)
1940s	24.3	30 (1.23)	5 (0.21)
1950s	24.5	34 (1.39)	7 (0.29)
1960s	24.0	28 (1.17)	11 (0.46)
1970s	23.8	10 (0.42)	8 (0.34)
1980s	25.3	25 (0.99)	6 (0.24)
1990s	27.9	37 (1.33)	17 (0.61)
2000s	29.6	48 (1.62)	15 (0.51)
Total		286	75

	Decade	No. of tokens	Frequency (per million words)
Table 2.2 Frequencies of non-sentential *of* NP complements in COHA from the 1860s to the 1950s			
	1860s	8	0.47
	1870s	4	0.22
	1880s	1	0.05
	1890s	2	0.10
	1900s	18	0.81
	1910s	29	1.28
	1920s	60	2.3
	1930s	54	2.2
	1940s	112	4.6
	1950s	71	2.9

the more frequent complement. However, from the 1910s onwards *of -ing* complements begin to be found in each decade alongside of *to* infinitives, and there is an overall rising trend in the frequency of *of -ing* complements from the 1940s onwards, with the construction becoming entrenched by the 1940s and the 1950s,[2] and the trend is especially noticeable in the two most recent decades. The rising trend is in accordance with the Great Complement Shift.

It was noted in Sect. 2.1 that the adjective *scared* also selects non-sentential *of* NP complements, and it is of interest to consider their incidence prior to, and during, the time when the sentential *of -ing* pattern was emerging and establishing itself. The period from the 1810s to the 1950s suggests itself for examination here. During the first five decades of this period there are virtually no *of* NP complements of *scared* in COHA, but such complements begin to occur from the 1860s onwards. Table 2.2 gives information on their frequency from the 1860s to the 1950s.

Comparing the findings presented in Table 2.2 with the findings on the sentential *of -ing* pattern in Table 2.1, it seems clear that the non-sentential pattern emerged and established itself somewhat earlier than the sentential pattern. Some tokens of the non-sentential pattern were encountered in the 1860s and the 1870s, and from the 1900s onwards it becomes established,[3] thus preceding the emergence and spread of the sentential pattern by some decades. The gerund is the most nouny of sentential complements, as has been shown in detail by Ross (2002), and the frequency of the *of* NP complement pattern may therefore have played a role in the spread of the gerundial pattern, against the background of the Great Complement Shift.

It is observed in Table 2.1 that it is in the period from the 1910s to the 2000s that both sentential complements are found with *scared* in consecutive decades, and for this reason the period in question is of central interest in the analysis of variation between the two patterns. There are 269 *to* infinitive and 74 *of-ing* complements in this period.

Turning to factors that may play a role in separating the two patterns in the case of the adjective *scared*, the Extraction Principle is a possible explanatory factor that is well-established in the literature by now.[4] It is a non-semantic factor, and it is relatively easy to apply. With respect to the present data, it is observed that some extractions of the type envisaged in the Extraction Principle are found in the period from the 1910s to the 2000s. Two examples are given in (6a–b).

(6)   a.   If I had some devilment I was scared to do myself, you know what   (1932,
           I'd do?   MAG)
      b.   I'd grown up there, tried everything I'd been scared to try till   (1977,
           then—I hated to think how …   FIC)

In both of (6a–b) the relevant extraction rule is Relativization, and the form of the complement is of the *to* infinitival type, as predicted by the Extraction Principle. However, the number of extractions overall is very low and among the well over 200 tokens being investigated from the 1910s to the 2000s there are only seven of them. (They are one each from the 1930s, 1940s, and 2000s and two each from the 1970s and 1990s.) All seven are of the *to* infinitival type, as predicted by the Extraction Principle. Given the well-established status of the Extraction Principle in work on complementation, it seems appropriate here to take note of the seven extractions and to set them aside when proceeding to the task of separating the two patterns from a semantic point of view.

When extractions are set aside, there remain 262 tokens of the *to* infinitival type alongside of the 74 tokens of the *of-ing* type in the period under investigation. In the literature a number of conceptual distinctions are found, and while a full survey of earlier work would not be appropriate here, it is helpful to mention one set of distinctions that can often be helpful. This is the one in Allerton (1988). According to him, the "infinitive-gerund distinction, in its healthy state, can be summed up" with the help of features given in Table 2.3.

The conceptual distinctions identified by Allerton do not always come to the surface in the two types of complement, and for instance with

Table 2.3 Conceptual distinctions pertinent to the infinitive-gerund distinction

Infinitive	Gerund
Infrequent activity	Regular activity
Intermittent activity	Continuous activity
Interrupted activity	Continuing activity
Uncompleted activity	Completed activity
Contingent/possible event	Event presented factually
Particular time and place	Neutral time and place
Specific subject	Non-specific subject
More verbal character	More nominal character

Source: Allerton (1988, 21)

respect to the last but one—the one relating to control—it is hard to see a difference in terms of control between the sentences in (1a–b) or those in (4a–b) and (5a–b). However, the distinctions in Allerton (1988) are often helpful, and the approach proposed here is meant to supplement earlier treatments, and it does not presume to replace them.

The approach that is proposed here is based on semantic roles or theta roles, and the focus is on the nature of the lower predicate and on the theta role that it assigns to the understood subject of the lower clause. The principle proposed has been termed the Choice Principle.

The Choice Principle
In the case of infinitival and gerundial complement options at a time of considerable variation between the two patterns, the infinitive tends to be associated with [+Choice] contexts and the gerund with [−Choice] contexts.

A [+Choice] context is defined in terms of agentivity in that a predicate that is agentive involves a [+Choice] context and a predicate that is non-agentive involves a [−Choice] context. Providing a solid definition of agentivity, in turn, is not necessarily an easy task. In the approach adopted here, agentivity has to do with the conceptualization and the presentation of events and states of affairs. A [+Choice] predicate with an agentive subject encodes an action, an event or a state of affairs in a way such that the referent of the subject of the sentence is presented as being volitionally involved in it, as exercising some degree of control over it, and as being in some degree responsible for it. These three concepts—volitional involvement, control, and responsibility—are here taken as key ingredients of agentive subjects and of [+Choice] contexts.[5] As for [−Choice] contexts, in their case the event or state of affairs in question is conceptualized as something happening to the referent of the subject, and the referent of the subject is not volitionally involved in the action, event or state of affairs (Rudanko 2012, 226). In the case of [−Choice] contexts, the concepts of "undergoing and having something happen to one," used by Thalberg (1967, 259) to analyze "verbs and verb phrases we use to report events in which a human being figures prominently," may be invoked.

The Choice Principle was first developed in a study of *to* infinitival and gerundial complements of the adjective *accustomed* in Rudanko (2010, 2011). To illustrate the [+/−Choice] distinction with this adjective, consider the sentences in (7a–b), which were cited from the TIME Corpus in Rudanko (2011, 133).

(7) a. The whole American people is becoming accustomed to eat Italian food. (1930)
     b. The eight directors were not men accustomed to be thus summarily   (1930)
         disposed of.

In sentence (7a) the predicate *eat Italian food* conceptualizes an event in such a way that the referent of the subject of the predicate is volitionally involved in the event, is in control of it and is responsible for it. By contrast, in (7b) the predicate *to be thus summarily disposed of* conceptualizes an event in such a way that the referent of the subject is not volitionally involved in the event, is not in control of it and is not responsible for it.

It may be added that [+Choice] predicates are natural in imperatives, while predicates whose subjects are low in agentivity or non-agentive are less natural in imperatives. This is because of a property of imperatives that has been succinctly summed up by Taylor:

> Prototypically, an imperative instructs a person to do something, and is therefore only acceptable if a person has a choice between carrying out the instruction or not. (Taylor 2003, 31)

From this perspective, it is possible to compare *Eat Italian food!*, which is entirely natural and likely as an imperative, and *?Be thus summarily disposed of!*, which is less likely as an imperative.

Agent oriented adverbs, including *deliberately* (cf. Givón 1993, 9) and purpose (or rationale) clauses, introduced for instance by *in order to* (Gruber 1967, 943; 1976, 161–162; Cruse 1973, 18–19) may also be considered when assessing whether a context is [+Choice] or [−Choice].

Thus, to begin with a [+Choice] context, sentences such as *They deliberately eat Italian food* and *They eat Italian food in order to stay healthy* are well formed, with agentive subjects and with the adverb and purpose clause connected to the subjects. As for [−Choice] contexts, sentences such as *They were deliberately disposed of thus summarily* and *They were disposed of thus summarily in order to streamline management* are also possible, but in them the adverb and the purpose clauses are connected to an understood or implicit Agent, not to the subjects of the sentences. That is, the surface subject *They* remains a Patient in both passive sentences. The understood Agent can of course be spelled out, as in *They were deliberately disposed of thus summarily by the shareholders in order to streamline management*. (For implicit arguments in passives and more generally in other constructions, see Roeper 1987.)

The Choice Principle was originally devised to explain variation between *to* infinitive and *to -ing* complements of the adjective *accustomed*, and since then it has also been applied to this variation in the case of other predicates (see for instance Rudanko 2012, 2017). The present study concerns a comparison of *to* infinitive and *of -ing* complements of the adjective *scared*. That is, the present study concerns a gerundial pattern that is different from the one selected by *accustomed*. It is then of interest to investigate whether the principle may shed light on the complement selection properties of the adjective *scared*.

Some illustrations of *to* infinitive and *of -ing* complements and [+/−Choice] environments are given in (8a–b) and (9a–b).

(8) a. ... we sat and held his bill, scared to open the envelope. (1919 MAG)

    b. I'm scared to be left alone in the room with it. (1913, FIC)

(9) a. She was scared of going upstairs where Sissie was. (1962, FIC)

    b. And Pa's as restless as a squirrel. All the time scared of losing his money. (1922, FIC)

The predicate *open the envelope*, as used in (8a), and the predicate *going upstairs*, as used in (9a), are [+Choice]. In these sentences the referents of the understood subjects are conceptualized as volitionally involved in the actions, in control of them and as responsible for them. By contrast, the predicate *be left alone in the room with it*, as used in (8b), and the predicate *losing his money*, as used in (9b), are [−Choice], and in these sentences the referents of the understood subjects are not conceptualized as being voli-

Table 2.4 Agentive and nonagentive contexts of *to* infinitive and *of*-*ing* complements of the adjective *scared* in the period from the 1910s to the 2000s

Decade	*to infinitives*		*of*-*ing*	
	[+Ch]	[−Ch]	[+Ch]	[−Ch]
1910s	13	2	1	
1920s	22	0	1	1
1930s	16	3	2	
1940s	28	1	2	3
1950s	32	2	5	2
1960s	26	2	4	7
1970s	8	0	3	5
1980s	24	1	2	4
1990s	28	7	10	7
2000s	40	7	6	9
Total	237	25	36	38

tionally involved in the events, nor in control of them, nor as responsible for them. Examples (8b) and (9b) illustrate how the concepts of "undergoing and having something happen to one" (Thalberg 1967, 259) are helpful to understanding the nature of non-agentive subjects.

It is clear from (8a–b) and (9a–b) that the Choice Principle cannot be a categorical rule in the case of the adjective *scared*. However, the question is whether it represents a significant tendency in the case of *scared*. For this purpose, the tokens in the present dataset were analyzed with respect to the Choice Principle. Table 2.4 gives information on agentive and nonagentive contexts of *to* infinitive and *of*-*ing* complements of the adjective *scared*.

The Chi Square for the total of the period in question is as high as 63.49, and the Choice Principle is significant at the level of $p < 0.0001$ (df = 1).

It is clear from Table 2.4 that of the four combinations the most frequent type by a long way has been, and continues to be, the *to* infinitive with a [+Choice] lower clause. Two further examples of this combination are given in (10a–b).

(10)   a.   She was scared to come back to school this noon.   (1954, FIC)
          b.   I was scared to stay in that huge, pretty hotel room ....   (2000, FIC)

As far as Old English is concerned, infinitival *to* has generally been analyzed as a preposition and the *to* infinitive has been viewed as a verbal noun

(Mitchell 1985, 387) or as "essentially nominal [...] but with already some verbal features incorporated" (Fischer 1996, 131; see also Los 2015, 144–145). However, in current English infinitival *to* is clearly verbal and the word *to* is under the Aux node in the approach outlined and motivated in Sect. 2.1. In spite of the change in syntax, the meaning of infinitival *to* can still be explicated on the basis of the preposition *to* in that it expresses movement toward a goal (Bolinger 1977, 151; Rudanko 1989, 35; Smith and Escobedo 2001, 552). Thus in (10a–b) the *to* infinitive clause has the role of Goal. The role of Goal goes well with the agentive interpretation of the lower clause.

As for *of* -*ing* complements, two further examples with [−Choice] lower clauses are given in (11a–b).

(11) a. In the 1930s, publishers were so scared of losing revenue to the   (1992,
        then-new radio industry ...   NEWS)
     b. We were scared of getting caught, especially by Stevie's dad.   (2004, FIC)

The preposition *of* can have varied meanings in current English, but its basic or original meaning has to do with removal or separation. The *Oxford English Dictionary* (*OED*) provides this comment:

> From its original sense, *of* was naturally used in the expression of the notions of removal, separation, privation, derivation, origin or source, starting-point, spring of action, cause, agent, instrument, material, and other senses, which involve the notion of "taking, coming, arising, or resulting from". (*OED*, s.v.)

The role of Source then suggests itself as a label for the lower clauses in (11a–b). The lower clause thus expresses the source of the state of fear or fright.[6] For instance, (11b) might be paraphrased along the lines of "we were in a state of fright that we might get caught."

With these remarks on the meaning of infinitival *to* and of the preposition *of* in mind, consider the sentences in (12a–b).

(12) a. And importantly, he wasn't scared of taking chances commercially   (1988,
        ...   NEWS)
     b. Most everyone she met used drugs and panhandled or stole ... or   (2004,
        worse. Scared of becoming like the haunted runaways she saw every   FIC)
        night at the shelter, and in the doorways, she searched frantically for
        odd jobs ...

The *of -ing* complements of *scared* again have the semantic role of Source. For instance, a gloss such as "In a state of fright that she would become like the haunted runaways" suggests itself for the key part of (12b). What is of interest then is to consider the *to* infinitive variants of the authentic sentences in (12a–b). These invented variants are given in (13a–b).

(13)   a.   And importantly, he wasn't scared to take chances commercially.
       b.   Most everyone she met used drugs and panhandled or stole … or worse. Scared to become like the haunted runaways she saw every night at the shelter, and in the doorways, she searched frantically for odd jobs …

To compare the *of -ing* and the *to* infinitive variants of the sentences, it is helpful to recall a comment made by Allerton (1988, 20) on comparing a *to* infinitive selected by an adjective and a corresponding gerundial construction consisting of a preposition and a gerund selected by the same adjective. He noted that when combined with a *to* infinitive complement, the adjective head may take on a more abstract meaning, but that in the gerundial construction the adjective preserves its basic meaning more fully. Allerton's point seems applicable to the comparison of (12a–b) and (13a–b). In the former, the adjective keeps its sense of "in a state of fright," but the *to* infinitive may suggest a slightly more abstract interpretation, with a touch of volition or control. Thus *scared to become like the haunted runaways* may suggest not wanting to become like the haunted runaways in (13b).

As for (13a), the key part of it seems close to "he was ready/prepared to take chances commercially." Rudanko (2015, 46–47) pointed to a sentence of the type "… she is apparently not afraid to be seen at less than her best," noting that the combination "*not + afraid + to* infinitive" may approach a stance marker in its function, conveying defiance in the face of a challenge. Such an interpretation may be appropriate for (13a). Overall, the ability of the *to* infinitive complement to suggest a more abstract sense for the adjective that selects the complement may go some way toward explaining the relatively high frequency of the *to* infinitive complement with *scared*.

One more observation may be added to the consideration of the Choice Principle and its relevance to the complements selected by the adjective *scared*. Above, it was pointed out that a passive lower clause is prototypically a [−Choice] context. The expectation is therefore that even though overall *of -ing* complements are much less frequent than *to* infinitives with *scared*, with passive lower clauses they may be more frequent than *to* infinitives. In the current dataset this expectation is borne out, for there are 13 sentences with passive lower clauses, and in nine of them the complement is indeed of the *of -ing* type and only in the remaining four is it a *to* infinitive.

The preponderance of *of -ing* complements over *to* infinitives in passive contexts in the present dataset is in accordance with the Choice Principle, but it is possible to probe the context of passive lower clauses a little further. For this purpose it is worth going beyond COHA briefly and reviewing data from COCA, the Corpus of Contemporary American English. This decision to consult a corpus of contemporary English seems justified because of the finding above that both *to* infinitives and *of -ing* complements were found to occur with a relatively high frequency in very recent English. The purpose is to target *to* infinitive and *of -ing* complements of the adjective where the lower clause is in the passive, and the specific search strings "scared to be [vʔn*]" and "scared of being [vʔn*]" suggest themselves for this purpose. These search strings retrieve nine *to* infinitives and as many as 26 *of -ing* complements. Three of the nine *to* infinitives turn out to be indirect complements, dependent on *too* rather than *scared*, and there are thus only six relevant *to* infinitives. These findings confirm the expectation that passive lower clauses, as a prototypical [−Choice] environment, tend to favor the *of -ing* complement in relation to *to* infinitives. Illustrations are given in (14a–b) and (15a–b).

(14) a. When the first day of school came, Romy was apprehensive, scared to be found out. But as the days went by, she didn't think about it at all.   (1997, FIC)

      b. The people are scared to come to our unit because they're scared to be seen here, and then it is basically declaring their status, ...   (2004, SPOK)

(15) a. I was so scared of being caught and having to go back.   (1990, NEWS)

      b. For the first time in my life I wasn't scared of being found out because for the first time I was fooling everybody.   (2013, FIC)

The lower predicates in the four sentences in (14a–b) and (15a–b) are in the passive and they are [−Choice]. The *of -ing* pattern is more frequent in this prototypically [−Choice] context, providing further support for the Choice Principle, but the *to* infinitives in (14a–b) are of course also authentic and well formed. It is therefore of interest to compare the two sets of sentences from the point of view of their meanings. It seems possible to say that the *to* infinitives in (14a–b) still have a slight touch of goal orientation and perhaps of control about them, which may suggest that the event of the lower clause may be imminent, as in (14a), with its reference to the first day of school. As for the *of -ing* complements in (15a–b) there is less goal orientation and the adjective retains its basic meaning of "in a state of fright" more purely. Such nuances of meaning naturally invite further investigation, but as regards the Choice Principle, the main point emerging from the data from COCA is the preponderance of *of -ing* complements in contexts of lower clause passives, as predicted by the principle, and the heuristic value of the principle in drawing attention to semantic contrasts between the two patterns in sentences with passive lower clauses.

2.3   *To* Infinitive and *of -ing* Complements of the Adjective *Scared* in the BNC

This section takes advantage of the comparability of the BNC to the section of COHA covering the last three decades of the twentieth century.[7] The comparison is carried out in order to determine whether the distribution of the *to* infinitive and the *of -ing* complements with *scared* in American English shows similarities to the distribution in British English. Aspects of interest include the relative proportions of *to* infinitive and *of -ing* complements, the occurrence of the passive lower clause in *of -ing* [−Choice] contexts, and levels of significance seen in the distribution of complements according to the Choice Principle, which, in American English, are highly significant.

The primary and supplementary search strings used for COHA were also used for the BNC search,[8] that is "scared to [vʔi*]," and "scared of [vʔg*]," for the *to* infinitive and the gerund respectively, plus allowances for the insertion of one or two words between *scared* and *to/of*, and the insertion of one word between *to* and the infinitive and between *of* and the gerund. The primary search string for the *to* infinitive returns a total of 118 tokens, and the supplementary searches turn up a further 18, giving a total of 136. Indirect complements account for as many as 63 of these tokens, and these are set aside, as are the small handful of irrelevant tokens resulting mostly from the supplementary search strings. The primary search string for the *of -ing* complement returns 44 tokens, and the supplementary searches add a further 13. Of this total of 57, only six need to be set aside as irrelevant. The total numbers of relevant tokens for *scared* obtained from the BYU-BNC are 63 *to* infinitive and 51 *of -ing* complements.

There are no cases of extraction evident in the BNC data, and the analysis thus proceeds to the application of the Choice Principle; the results are given in Table 2.5.

The Chi Square is 32.55, and is significant at the level of $p < 0.0001$ (df = 1). This allows the suggestion that the Choice Principle has a highly significant effect on non-finite complement choice in the case of *scared* in recent British English. Examples of [+Choice] and [−Choice] contexts in the BNC are given in (16a–b) and (17a–b) below.

(16) a. He said he had been scared to tell the truth after a series of   (K5M 4091)
         threats from one of the gang.
     b. ...the women came to the factory beaten by their husbands and   (F9S 565)
         how some were scared to be downgraded in their work because
         they feared a beating from husbands...
(17) a. Was he simply scared of committing himself once again, in fear of (JY4 2852)
         a second rejection?
     b. ...a motorist who refused a breath test because he was scared of   (CBF 9553)
         catching Aids...

(16a) and (17a) are illustrations of [+Choice] lower clauses with each of the two complement types, while (16b) and (17b) are [−Choice] examples with both complements.

One feature of the numbers given in Table 2.5 recalls a comment made in connection with Table 2.4—that of the four categories, *to* infinitive [+/−Choice] and *of -ing* [+/−Choice], the one that attracts the highest frequencies is the *to* infinitive with a [+Choice] lower clause in American English. The indication is that the connection between the infinitival complement and the [+Choice] context is also strong in British English. One aspect of the numbers in Table 2.5 that might signal a difference in complement selection tendencies between the two varieties, however, is seen

Table 2.5   [+Choice] and [−Choice] contexts of *to* infinitive and *of -ing* complements of the adjective *scared* in the BNC

	[+Choice]	*[−Choice]*	*Total*
to infinitives	59	4	63
of -ing complements	22	29	51

Table 2.6   A comparison of [+Choice] and [−Choice] contexts with *scared* in the BNC and COHA 1970s–1990s (77 million words)

Corpus	to infinitives		of -ing	
	[+Ch]	*[−Ch]*	*[+Ch]*	*[−Ch]*
BNC	59 (0.59)	4 (0.04)	22 (0.22)	29 (0.29)
COHA	60 (0.78)	8 (0.10)	15 (0.19)	16 (0.21)

in the high frequency of gerundial complements in relation to *to* infinitives. Given that a far higher share of the overall data from COHA was taken up by the *to* infinitive, this is something of interest, and will be returned to in the comparison of the two datasets below.

In accordance with the earlier observation that passive lower clauses are more likely to occur with *of -ing* complements in [−Choice] contexts than any other type, the BNC data show four passives found with *of -ing* complements, and two with *to* infinitives, one of which is (16b) above. All six of the BNC passive tokens are of the [−Choice] type.

Table 2.6 provides the results of the comparison of the BNC data to that of the relevant decades of COHA in the application of the Choice Principle. The three decades of COHA that lend themselves to this comparison, the 1970s, 1980s and 1990s, amount to 77 million words, while the BNC is 100 million words. Normalized frequencies are thus provided in parentheses.

The Chi Square for this section of COHA is 16.3 ($p < 0.0001$, df = 1) (it will be recalled that the Chi Square for the BNC was 32.55 [$p < 0.0001$, df = 1]). Both datasets thus show a highly significant correlation between complement choice and the predictions made by the Choice Principle. To the extent that the data in Table 2.6 allow, it can also be suggested that the overall frequency of the *of -ing* complement in British English is higher than that of American English. Further study using more directly comparable corpora will naturally be desirable on this issue against the backdrop of the Great Complement Shift.

2.4   Concluding Observations

The present chapter traces *to* infinitive and *of -ing* complements of the adjective *scared* in American English over the last two centuries, and provides a comparison with the British English of recent decades. In terms of American English, it was observed that both types of construction are very rare with the adjective in the nineteenth century, and that those complements that do occur are mostly of the *to* infinitive type. In the early decades of the twentieth century *to* infinitives rose in frequency, and they continued to be more frequent than *of* -*ing* complements throughout the century. Still the *of* -*ing* complement began to emerge in the twentieth century, reaching a normalized frequency of 0.61 and 0.51 per million words in the two most recent decades. The normalized frequency of the *to* infinitive is clearly higher in the same decades at about 1.33 or 1.62, and there is no sign of the *of* -*ing* pattern supplanting the *to* infinitive with the predicate under consideration in American English. Even so, the rise of the *of* -*ing* pattern is in the spirit of the Great Complement Shift.

The two non-finite complements are not very different from the point of view of their meanings, and under such circumstances the key task is to identify factors that bear on complement choice. The Extraction Principle is a syntactic generalization that has been found to be such a factor in earlier work, but in the present case the number of extractions turned out to be low. The Choice Principle is a semantic factor that has been proposed very recently, and the present study examined its relevance to the complement selection properties of the adjective *scared*, finding that it is worth considering as a factor. The comparison with data from recent British English helped to strengthen the argument for the viability of the Choice Principle as a tool for determining complement selection tendencies in adjectival predicates, and a high level of statistical significance is evident in both the American and British English data. With the comparison of the BNC to the recent decades of COHA, it was seen that the gerundial complement of *scared* may be used with more frequency in British English than it is in American English, thus suggesting, pending further work, that with this adjective the effect of the Great Complement Shift may be at a more advanced stage in British English.

With respect to the Choice Principle, the authors would not presume to claim that the principle is always applicable to explain complement selection properties of predicates that select *to* infinitives and gerundial complements, but the present investigation invites further work on the applicability of the Choice Principle in cases of such variation.

NOTES

1. It might be tempting to argue that sentences with insertions are explained by the Complexity Principle, associating a more explicit variant with a more complex environment (see Rohdenburg 1996). *To* infinitives are unques-

tionably more explicit that non-prepositional gerunds, but in light of Rohdenburg (1995, 75) and Vosberg (2006, 63, 175), it is not clear whether insertions can be accounted for by the Complexity Principle when comparing *to* infinitives and prepositional gerunds, because the latter are more explicit than non-prepositional gerunds. It may also be mentioned that Tyrkkö and Rudanko (forthcoming) did not find that insertions are a significant factor favoring *to* infinitives over a prepositional gerund pattern. Pending further work on this issue, it is safest not to argue that insertions are explained by the Complexity Principle, since the present comparison concerns *to* infinitives and gerunds introduced by a preposition.

2. In this connection it is of interest to quote Goldberg on her notion of a construction:

> Any linguistic pattern is recognized as a construction as long as some aspect of its form or function is not strictly predictable from its component parts or from other constructions recognized to exist. In addition, patterns are stored as constructions even if they are fully predictable as long as they occur with sufficient frequency ... (Goldberg 2006, 5)

As is clear from Chap. 1 and Sect. 2.1 of the present chapter, the framework of analysis used in the present book differs from Goldberg's in a number of respects. For instance, the present authors do not espouse Goldberg's view of syntactic form as "what you see is what you get" (Goldberg 2006, 10; see also Goldberg 2013, 15), for reasons given in Chap. 1 and in Sect. 2.1 of the present chapter. Further, the present authors believe, in line with much other work, that extraction rules (see also Postal 1994) are well motivated in shedding light on the syntax of certain types of sentences, including *wh* questions, relative clauses and topicalized sentences (see for instance Radford 1997, 267–268; Huddleston and Pullum 2002, 1080; Brinton and Brinton 2010, 256–257). Extraction rules also make it possible to formulate generalizations of the type of the Extraction Principle, introduced in Chap. 1. Such a principle would presumably be incompatible with one aspect of Goldberg's framework, since for her, "[g]rammar does not involve any transformational or derivational component" (Goldberg 2013, 15). However, in spite of such differences, the basic notion of a construction in Goldberg's work as a pairing or combination of form and meaning (Goldberg 1995, 1) can still be valuable, and Goldberg's point about frequency of occurrence is also worth bearing in mind. No precise rule can be given on what constitutes a sufficient frequency for a string of elements to count as a construction—on the difficulty of operationalizing the concept of sufficient frequency, see Traugott and Trousdale (2013, 11)—but the investigator can be guided by a judgment on what is likely to yield some worthwhile generalization. In the present case, a frequency of two tokens in a corpus of over 24 million words, as in the 1930s, seems low, but five tokens in the 1940s and the rising trend that follows suggest a construction that is entrenching itself and is worth investigating.

3. With respect to the nineteenth century, it may be noted that the adjective *scared*, in its different uses, was relatively rare in the early years of the century. For the 1820s, for instance, the present investigators only found 14 tokens (2.03 per million words) of the adjective. In the course of the nineteenth century the adjective became much more frequent, and for instance for the 1880s the present investigators counted 121 (5.9 per million words) adjectival uses of *scared*. However, it still took another two decades before *of* NP complements began to be regularly found in a more noteworthy fashion.

4. Rohdenburg (2016) is a recent and wide-ranging investigation of extractions out of sentential complements. For the purposes of the present study, it is worth noting Rohdenburg's general conclusion that the "marked infinitive [...] enjoys a privileged or target status in extraction contexts"—Rohdenburg's term "marked infinitive" corresponds to the *to* infinitive used in the present study—and that the *to* infinitive "outranks all kinds of gerunds" in such contexts (2016, 481; for discussion see pp. 474–475 of the article). These conclusions are in accordance with the Extraction Principle, which can be regarded as spelling out the aspect of extractions that is relevant to comparing *to* infinitives and gerunds.

5. The term "volitional involvement" goes back to Dowty (1991, 572), who used the fuller phrase "volitional involvement in the event or state" in his comments on what he called the Agent Proto-Role. Other classic studies of agentivity and of the Agent role include Gruber (1967) and Lakoff (1977). The former observed that an "[a]gentive verb is one whose subject refers to an animate object which is thought of as the willful source or agent of the activity described in the sentence" (1967, 943), and the latter considered what he termed "prototypical agent-patient" sentences and offered a long list of properties that such sentences have in "prototypical uses" (1977, 244). Some of these are of limited applicability, including no. 14 on the list ("the agent is looking at the patient"), but the three properties highlighted in the text have equivalents or near equivalents in Lakoff's list. For instance, as regards "volitional involvement," Lakoff's formulation (his property 4) is: "the agent's action is volitional" (Lakoff 1977, 244). The three properties highlighted as properties of agentivity in the text are also prominent in Hundt's (2004, 49) discussion of Agents and agentivity.

6. As noted in Sect. 2.1, the adjective *scared* often selects *of* NP complements, and the source-like interpretation of the complement is often clear in their case. Consider (ia–b) from COHA:

(i)   a.   You're not scared of snakes are you?   (1964, FIC)
      b.   I'm scared of that Lacey.   (1944, FIC)

For instance, sentence (ib) has the approximate meaning "I am afraid of what that Lacey may do to me," where the *of* NP complement expresses the source of the fear. The interpretation of the *of* NP complement seems reminiscent of a [−Choice] context, in that the construction is about what may happen to the referent of the subject. This semantic similarity may also have played a part in the spread of the sentential *of-ing* complements of the [−Choice] variety.

7. The BNC contains material spanning the period 1960–1993. The majority of written material was published during the last 10 years or so of that period. This should be borne in mind, but in the absence of a corpus of British English that would match COHA more fully, here we use the two corpora to shed at least some light on the regional varieties in question.

8. The BNC can be accessed in a few different ways, and the version we chose to use for *scared* was the BYU-BNC. During the data collection process it was noticed that there are often some small differences in the number of tokens retrieved using different versions of the BNC; often the BYU-BNC returns a small number of tokens more, or fewer, than the BNCweb CQP edition, but the differences are minor in the case of a relatively frequent adjective such as *scared*, and we were satisfied with the results from the BYU-BNC.

REFERENCES

Allerton, David J. 1988. 'Infinitivitis' in English. In *Essays on the English Language and Applied Linguistics on the Occasion of Gerhard Nickel's 60th Birthday*, ed. Josef Klegraf and Dietrich Nehls, 11–23. Heidelberg: Groos.

Bolinger, Dwight. 1968. Entailment and the Meaning of Structures. *Glossa* 2: 119–127.

———. 1977. *Meaning and Form*. London: Longman.

Brinton, Laurel J., and Donna M. Brinton. 2010. *The Linguistic Structure of Modern English*. Amsterdam and Philadelphia: John Benjamins.

Chomsky, Noam. 1981. *Lectures on Government and Binding*. Dordrecht: Foris.

———. 1986. *Knowledge of Language: Its Nature, Origin and Use*. New York: Praeger.

Cruse, D.A. 1973. Some Thoughts on Agentivity. *Journal of Linguistics* 9: 11–23.

Dowty, David. 1991. Thematic Proto-roles and Argument Selection. *Language* 67: 547–619.

Fischer, Olga. 1996. The Status of *to* in Old English *to*-infinitives. *Lingua* 99: 107–133.

Givón, Talmy. 1993. *English Grammar: A Function-based Introduction. Volume II*. Amsterdam and Philadelphia: John Benjamins.

Goldberg, Adele. 1995. *Constructions. A Construction Grammar Approach to Argument Structure.* Chicago: University of Chicago Press.
———. 2006. *Constructions at Work.* Oxford: Oxford University Press.
———. 2013. Constructionist Approaches. In *The Oxford Handbook of Construction Grammar*, ed. Thomas Hoffman and Graeme Trousdale, 15–31. Oxford: Oxford University Press.
Gruber, Jeffrey S. 1967. Look and See. *Language* 43 (4): 937–947.
———. 1976. *Lexical Structures in Syntax and Semantics.* Amsterdam: North-Holland Publishing Company.
Huddleston, Rodney, and Geoffrey Pullum. 2002. *The Cambridge Grammar of the English Language.* Cambridge: Cambridge University Press.
Hundt, Marianne. 2004. Animacy, Agentivity, and the Spread of the Progressive in Modern English. *English Language and Linguistics* 8: 47–69.
Jespersen, Otto. [1940] 1961. *A Modern English Grammar on Historical Principles. Part V: Syntax* (Vol. IV). London: Allen and Unwin.
Lakoff, George. 1977. Linguistic Gestalts. In *Papers from the Thirteenth Regional Meeting of the Chicago Linguistics Society*, ed. Woodford A. Beach, Samuel E. Fox, and Shulamith Philosoph, 236–287. Chicago: Chicago Linguistics Society.
Los, Bettelou. 2015. *A Historical Syntax of English.* Edinburgh: Edinburgh University Press.
Mitchell, Bruce. 1985. *Old English Syntax.* Vol. 1. Oxford: Clarendon Press.
Oxford Advanced Learner's Dictionary of Current English. 2005. 7th ed. Oxford: Oxford University Press.
Oxford English Dictionary. 1989. 2nd ed. OED Online. Oxford: Oxford University Press. Accessed February 2017. http://www.oed.com
Postal, Paul. 1994. Contrasting Extraction Types. *Journal of Linguistics* 30: 159–186.
Quirk, Randolph, Sidney Greenbaum, Geoffrey Leech, and Jan Svartvik. 1985. *A Comprehensive Grammar of the English Language.* London: Longman.
Radford, Andrew. 1997. *Syntactic Theory and the Structure of English.* Cambridge: Cambridge University Press.
Roeper, Thomas. 1987. Implicit Arguments and the Head-complement Relation. *Linguistic Inquiry* 18 (2): 267–310.
Rohdenburg, Günter. 1995. Beiträge zum Auf- und Abstieg einiger präpositioneller Konstruktionen im Englisch. *Nowele* 26: 67–124.
———. 1996. Cognitive Complexity and Increased Grammatical Explicitness in English. *Cognitive Linguistics* 7: 149–182.
———. 2016. Tracking Two Processing Principles with Respect to the Extraction of Elements Out of Complement Clauses in English. *English Language and Linguistics* 20: 463–486.
Ross, John Robert. 2002. Nouniness. In *Fuzzy Grammar*, ed. Bas Aarts, David Denison, Evelien Keizer, and Gergana Popova, 351–422. Oxford: Oxford University Press.

Rudanko, Juhani. 1989. *Complementation and Case Grammar*. Albany, NY: SUNY Press.

———. 2010. Explaining Grammatical Variation and Change: A Case Study of Complementation in American English over Three Decades. *Journal of English Linguistics* 38: 4–24.

———. 2011. *Changes in Complementation in British and American English: Corpus-based Studies on Non-finite Complements in Recent English*. Basingstoke: Palgrave Macmillan.

———. 2012. Exploring Aspects of the Great Complement Shift, with Evidence from the TIME Corpus and COCA. In *The Oxford Handbook of the History of English*, ed. Terttu Nevalainen and Elizabeth Closs Traugott, 222–232. Oxford: Oxford University Press.

———. 2015. *Linking Form and Meaning: Studies on Selected Control Patterns in Recent English*. Basingstoke: Palgrave Macmillan.

———. 2017. *Infinitives and Gerunds in Recent English: Studies on Non-Finite Complements with Data from Large Corpora*. London: Palgrave Macmillan Springer.

Smith, Michael B., and Joyce Escobedo. 2001. The Semantics of *to*-infinitival vs. *-ing* Verb Complement Constructions in English. In *Proceedings from the Main Session of the Chicago Linguistic Society's Thirty-seventh Meeting*, ed. Mary Andronis, Christopher Ball, Heidi Elston, and Sylvain Neuvel, 549–563. Chicago: Chicago Linguistic Society.

Taylor, John R. 2003. Meaning and Context. In *Motivation in Language. Studies in Honor of Günter Radden*, ed. Hubert Cuyckens, Thomas Berg, René Dirven, and Klaus-Uwe Panther, 27–48. Amsterdam: John Benjamins.

Thalberg, Irving. 1967. Verbs, Deeds and What Happens to Us. *Theoria* 33: 259–277.

Traugott, Elizabeth, and Graeme Trousdale. 2013. *Constructionalization and Constructional Changes*. Oxford: Oxford University Press.

Tyrkkö, Jukka, and Juhani Rudanko. forthcoming. ms. Grammar, Text Type, and Diachrony as Factors Influencing Complement Choice. Submitted for publication in Merja Kytö and Lucia Siebers (eds.), *Earlier North American Englishes*.

Vosberg, Uwe. 2003. The Role of Extractions and *horror aequi* in the Evolution of *-ing* Complements in Modern English. In *Determinants of Grammatical Variation in English*, ed. Günter Rohdenburg and Britta Mondorf, 305–327. Berlin: Mouton de Gruyter.

———. 2006. *Die grosse Komplementverschiebung*. Tübingen, Germany: Narr.

Semantic Roles and Complement Selection: A Case Study of the Adjective *Terrified*

Abstract Chapter 3 investigates the distribution of the two non-finite complement options, the *to* infinitive and *of -ing*, as selected by the adjective *terrified* in recent American English and British English. Data from COHA, dating back to the 1840s, provides a first glimpse into the beginnings of non-finite complement use with *terrified* in recent English, and is supplemented with data on the early twenty-first century from COCA to provide a more complete picture of American English usage patterns. The data is considered against the general principles of the Great Complement Shift and the Extraction Principle. As in Chap. 2, the main goal of the present chapter is to further probe the relevance of the Choice Principle, and the data is then categorized on the basis of the Principle; the level of agentivity inherent in the lower clause predicate. British English data, from the BNC, is then introduced, and the results of the application of the aforementioned theoretical tools are compared in the two main varieties.

Keywords Subject control • Choice Principle • COHA • COCA • BNC

P. Rickman, J. Rudanko, *Corpus-Based Studies on Non-Finite Complements in Recent English*, https://doi.org/10.1007/978-3-319-72989-3_3

3.1   INTRODUCTION

This chapter continues the theme of Chap. 2 in that it deals with *to* infinitive and *of-ing* complements with adjectival predicates, but this time the matrix predicate being investigated is the adjective *terrified*. Initial illustrations of the two patterns with this adjective are given in (1a–b), which are from COHA.

(1)   a.   He really was terrified to tell you.   (1981, FIC)
       b.   … she was terrified of telling her children.   (1997, MAG)

The predicate of the matrix clause is the adjective *terrified* in (1a–b), and it assigns a theta role to the subject of its clause. The lower clause in (1a–b) has an understood subject, for reasons discussed in Chap. 1, and the two patterns are subject control constructions, with the higher subject controlling the understood subject, represented with the symbol PRO in current work. The *of* of the *of-ing* pattern is of course a preposition and as regards the *to* of the *to* infinitive complement, VP Deletion constructions can again, as in Chap. 2, be used to motivate placing infinitival *to* under the Aux node. In support, it can be noted that there is a contrast between the sentences in (2a–b), modified from the authentic sentences in (1a–b).

(2)   a.   He really was terrified to tell you, but his friend was not terrified to.
       b.   *She was terrified of telling her children but her friend was not terrified of.

The structures of (1a–b) can then be represented in their relevant aspects as in (1a′–b′).

(1)   a′.   [[He]$_{NP}$ really was [[terrified]$_{Adj}$ [[PRO]$_{NP}$ [to]$_{Aux}$ [tell you]$_{VP}$]$_{S2}$]$_{AdjP}$]$_{S1}$
       b′.   [[She]$_{NP}$ was [[terrified]$_{Adj}$ [[of]$_{Prep}$ [[[PRO]$_{NP}$ [telling her children]$_{VP}$]$_{S2}$]$_{NP}$]$_{PP}$]$_{AdjP}$]$_{S1}$

As regards the treatment of the adjective in standard dictionaries, the 7th edition of the *OALD* (2005) provides the gloss "very frightened" and gives an illustration of what are here termed *of-ing* complements under this sense, alongside of *that* clauses and *of* NP complements. However, *to* infinitives are not mentioned. For its part, the 8th edition of the *Collins Cobuild Advanced Learner's Dictionary* (2014) illustrates *of* NP complements and *that* clause complements, and also mentions *to* infinitive complements, but does not illustrate them. As for the *OED*, the relevant sense is sense 1:

1.   Seized with terror; affected or attended by terror. In predicative use freq. with *of.*

Of NP complements are found among the illustrations of the adjective *terrified* in the *OED*, but sentential complements are not found among them.

Overall, this brief survey of the treatment of the adjective in the dictionaries consulted here sheds light on aspects of the meaning and use of the adjective *terrified*, but the accounts also suggest that a more detailed study of *to* infinitive and *of*-*ing* complements of *terrified* is warranted. It is the purpose of the present study first of all to provide a descriptive account of the use of the two variants of sentential complement selected by the adjective *terrified* in recent English. For this purpose COHA is a natural source of data, because of its size and generally balanced nature. A point of interest here is the relation of the complementation of the adjective *terrified* to the Great Complement Shift. A further major objective is to inquire whether the Extraction Principle and the Choice Principle can shed light on the argument structure properties of the adjective *terrified*. To achieve this objective, the authors consider data from COHA, and in order to shed further light on usage in very recent English in the two main varieties of English, they also analyze a major segment of COCA, and the BNC.

3.2   *To* Infinitive and *of*-*ing* Complements of the Adjective *Terrified* in COHA

To collect tokens of *to* infinitive and *of*-*ing* complements of the adjective *terrified* in COHA, the search strings "terrified to [vʔi*]" and "terrified of [vʔg*]" suggest themselves, analogously to the search strings used in Chap. 2. These retrieve 98 *to* infinitives and 58 *of*-*ing* complements. The search strings are good in terms of precision, and most of these tokens are relevant, except that in the case of *to* infinitives, there are a largish number of indirect complements—51 out of the total 98—where the complement is linked to *too* in front of the adjective. Two examples are given in (3a–b).

(3) a. Poor Jacob was too terrified to understand of what crime he had   (1892, FIC)
         been accused.
     b. I was far too terrified to suggest any better course. ...   (1913,
                                                                       MAG)

Indirect complements of the type of (3a–b) are found fairly frequently in some decades, and for instance both in the 1890s and 1910s there are five of them retrieved with the basic search string for *to* infinitives. Indirect complements are not immediately relevant, but their presence deserves to be noted.

The basic search strings were supplemented in the same way as those in Chap. 2 with searches making provision for one or two words between *terrified* and *to/of* and for one word between *to* and the infinitive and between *of* and the *-ing* form. The supplementary search strings retrieved four relevant additional tokens, two of which are given in (4a–b).

(4) a. ... dreaming while she slept that she was awake and terrified of never   (1969,
         being able to sleep ...   FIC)
     b. ... he had to maintain sufficient dignity so that no one would suspect   (1972,
         how terrified he was of tripping up   FIC)

Table 3.1 gives information on the incidence of *to* infinitive and *of -ing* complements of the adjective *terrified* in COHA. The table begins with the 1840s, because no tokens of either pattern were encountered in earlier decades of the corpus, and it also omits the decades of the 1880s and the 1890s because no tokens were encountered in these decades either. Numbers in parentheses indicate frequencies normalized to words per million.

The figures in Table 3.1 and the graphic representation given in Fig. 3.1 show that only *to* infinitives were encountered in the nineteenth century, and that even these were very rare in that century. *Of -ing* complements began to be found in the 1930s, and overall their frequency maintained itself or showed a rise in the course of the century. The rise became more noticeable in the two most recent decades of the corpus.[1] For their part, the frequency of *to* infinitives also showed a rise in the last two—or three—most recent decades. On the other hand, the generally low frequency of *to* infinitives in earlier decades may go some way toward explaining why the *to* infinitive pattern has been neglected in some standard dictionaries. The increasing frequency of the pattern means that it should be recognized in current English.

Table 3.1 The incidence of *to* infinitive and *of*-*ing* complements with *terrified* in COHA

	Size	to infinitives	of -ing
1840s	16.0	1 (0.06)	
1850s	16.5	2 (0.12)	
1860s	17.1	1 (0.06)	
1870s	18.6	1 (0.05)	
1900s	22.1	3 (0.14)	
1910s	22.7	1 (0.04)	
1920s	25.7	3 (0.12)	
1930s	24.6	4 (0.16)	3 (0.12)
1940s	24.3		2 (0.08)
1950s	24.5	1 (0.04)	4 (0.16)
1960s	24.0	2 (0.08)	8 (0.33)
1970s	23.8	2 (0.08)	7 (0.29)
1980s	25.3	6 (0.24)	6 (0.24)
1990s	27.9	10 (0.36)	13 (0.47)
2000s	29.6	12 (0.41)	17 (0.57)

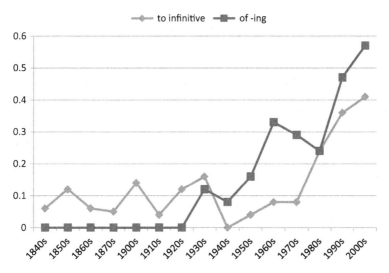

Fig. 3.1 The incidence of *to* infinitive and *of*-*ing* complements with *terrified* in COHA

Comparing the descriptive findings on the adjective *terrified* with those on the adjective *scared*, both show a clear rise in the frequency of the gerundial pattern in the course of the twentieth century, which is in the spirit of the Great Complement Shift. As far as the adjective *terrified* is concerned, the rise has been more pronounced in comparison with *to* infinitives, and it is noticeable that the gerundial pattern occurs with a slightly higher frequency in four of the five most recent decades of the corpus. At the same time, the overall frequencies of the two patterns remain fairly low, and even though they are clearly rising, they generally remain well below the corresponding frequencies of the two patterns in the case of the adjective *scared*, as discussed in Chap. 2.

The frequencies of the two non-finite patterns are fairly low in COHA, but the figures in Table 3.1 nevertheless testify to grammatical variation between the two patterns, especially in recent English. It is therefore possible to investigate whether the Extraction Principle and the Choice Principle may be used to explain variation between the two patterns. Given the evidence of Table 3.1 it seems appropriate to study the question in the period from the 1950s to the 2000s, since during this period both patterns are found in each consecutive decade.

As far as the Extraction Principle is concerned, it appears to be of limited applicability in the present case. The reason is simply that there do not appear to be any extractions in the sense of the Extraction Principle as introduced in Chap. 2 in the dataset from the 1950s to the 2000s. On the other hand, the Choice Principle can be considered at greater length. The comments on identifying agentive and non-agentive predicates that were presented in Chap. 2 can be taken for granted here, and it is clear that both types of lower predicates are found in complements of the adjective *terrified*. The examples in (5a–b) and (6a–b) can be considered as illustrations.

(5) a. Any gentleman in his right mind would be terrified to venture in this area of the city, rife with thieves' kitchens. (1999, FIC)

b. … he was terrified to hear the snap of some huge creature's jaws near him. (1918, FIC)

(6) a. I knew that she was terrified of touching one cent of the capital, … (1959, FIC)

b. Middle managers will continue to lose their jobs in a decentralized corporation—or be terrified of losing them. (1992, MAG)

Table 3.2 [+Choice] and [−Choice] interpretations of *to* infinitive and *of*-*ing* complements of *terrified* from the 1950s to the 2000s

Decade	to infinitives		of-ing	
	[+Choice]	*[−Choice]*	*[+Choice]*	*[−Choice]*
1950s		1	1	3
1960s	1	1		8
1970s		2		7
1980s	6		5	1
1990s	7	3	7	6
2000s	11	1	6	11
Total	25	8	19	36

The predicates *venture in this area of the city* ..., as used in (5a), and *touching one cent of the capital,* as used in (6a), are agentive. They encode a conceptualization of an action or event such that the referent of the understood subject is volitionally involved in it, exerts control over it, and is responsible for it. By contrast, the predicates *hear the snap of some huge creature's jaws near him,* as used in (5b), and *losing them,* as used in (6b), are non-agentive.[2] They encode events that happen to the referent of the understood subject or that the referent of the understood subject undergoes, such that the referent of the understood subject is neither volitionally involved in the events, nor in control of them, nor responsible for them.

It is clear from (5b) and (6a) that the Choice Principle cannot be a categorical rule in the case of the adjective *terrified,* but it is of interest to see if it represents a significant tendency in the present dataset. Table 3.2 gives information on the [+Choice] and [−Choice] interpretations of *to* infinitive and *of*-*ing* complements from the 1950s to the 2000s.

Applying the Chi Square test, the Chi square is 12.41 and the results are significant at the level of $p < 0.001$ (df = 1).

3.3 *To* INFINITIVE AND *OF*-*ING* COMPLEMENTS OF THE ADJECTIVE *TERRIFIED* IN COCA

It was observed in Sect. 3.2 that the Choice Principle is a significant factor bearing on variation between *to* infinitive and *of*-*ing* complements of the adjective *terrified* in the COHA dataset of recent English. However, as was noted, the numbers of tokens are fairly low in COHA, and it is therefore appropriate to turn to a second corpus for further analysis of the two non-finite complement patterns selected by the adjective. COCA suggests itself for this purpose because it is a large corpus of very recent English, and, as was seen in Table 3.1, the two patterns show their highest frequency of occurrence in very recent English. To gain information on very recent English, the period from 2000 to 2015 in COCA is considered here. One point of interest here is to find out if the slightly higher frequency of the *of -ing* pattern in relation to *to* infinitives in very recent English is confirmed in a larger corpus. From a more theoretical perspective, the status of the Choice Principle in the larger dataset also deserves further investigation.

The same search strings can be used as were used in the case of COHA. The basic search strings retrieve the overwhelming majority of tokens, but the supplementary search strings bring in six additional *to* infinitives and seven additional *of -ing* complements. Two illustrations of tokens retrieved with the supplementary search strings are given in (7a–b).

(7) a. We are indeed profoundly terrified to truly face the traumas of   (2008,
       our history.   ACAD)
    b. She is terrified of not being loved.   (2005,
                                                                             SPOK)

With respect to their precision, the basic search strings and the supple-mentary search strings work well. Admittedly, they retrieve a largish num-ber of indirect complements, of the type illustrated in (3a–b), but these are easily excluded manually.

The total of relevant *to* infinitive complements retrieved from the period under review in COCA is 84[3] and the corresponding number of *of -ing* complements is 158. These numbers provide clear evidence for the sug-gestion, made on the basis of COHA above, that in very recent English the *of -ing* pattern has become more frequent with the adjective *terrified* than the *to* infinitive pattern. This is in accordance with the Great Complement Shift.

Turning to the Extraction Principle and the Choice Principle as factors to explain variation between the two nonfinite complementation patterns, it is observed with respect to the Extraction Principle that extractions in the sense of the principle are very rare in the data from COCA, as they were in the data from COHA. Only three tokens with extraction were found. These are given in (8a–c).

(8) a. ...a strange sort of complacency, an ease that he was now terrified to   (2007,
remember.   FIC)
b. ... willing to take more aggressively redistributionist economic   (2011,
positions that Republicans despise and Democrats are terrified of   MAG)
espousing, if indeed they believe them at all.
c. She was brimming with pent up emotion which she was terrified of   (2001,
spilling in case I wouldn't take her seriously.   FIC)

In view of the well-established status of the Extraction Principle, the three tokens with extraction are set aside from further consideration. The low number of extractions makes it all the more appropriate to probe the role of the Choice Principle in the present dataset.

Table 3.3 gives information on the frequencies of [+Choice] and [−Choice] complements in COCA in the period from 2000 to 2015.

The Chi square is as high as 45.68 and the results are significant at the level of $p < 0.0001$ (df = 1).

Some illustrations from COCA are given in (9a–b) and (10a–b).

(9)   a. People are terrified to go outdoors, and lots of people are leaving   (2014,
areas close to the border ...   SPOK)
b. ... read that I am a Mormon and think that I hate gay people. I am   (2004,
terrified to be judged in this city because of it.   MAG)
(10) a. She is terrified of going somewhere new simply to end up invisible   (2013,
again.   FIC)
b. Terrified of losing him, Zarya breathed in his warm masculine   (2012,
scent.   FIC)

In (9a) and (10a) the lower predicates are [+Choice]. For instance, the referent of the understood subject of the predicate *go outdoors*, as used in (9a), is conceived of as being volitionally involved in the action, as being in control of it, and as being responsible for it. By contrast, the predicates *be judged in this city* and *losing him*, as used in (9b) and (10b), respectively,

Table 3.3 [+Choice] and [−Choice] complements of the adjective *terrified* in COCA from 2000 to 2015

	[+Choice]	*[−Choice]*	*Total*
to infinitives	66	17	83
of-*ing* complements	51	105	156

are [−Choice], and the referents of their understood subjects are not volitionally involved in the events in question. Neither are they in control of them, nor responsible for them. In the case of (9b), the lower predicate is a passive infinitive, and the understood subject corresponds to the direct object of the active version of the sentence, and has the role of Patient or Undergoer, which is at the opposite end of the spectrum from an Agent. A passive lower predicate is a prototypical [−Choice] environment.

The judgments on the nature of the lower predicates in (9a–b) and (10a–b) are fairly easy to make, but when making them it is important to pay attention to the context of the predicate. For a further example, consider sentence (11), where some larger context is provided.

(11) Although her vision was sometimes affected, she managed to compensate   (2013,
      at work because both eyes were rarely impaired simultaneously. The   NEWS)
      ophthalmologist, she said, was unmoved by her account. He told her she
      was being "emotional" and made it clear he believed she was
      exaggerating. Keep using the drops, he advised. Bream, devastated that
      the doctor thought she was being a drama queen, vowed never to return.
      For much of the next year, she used the drops every few hours round the
      clock—she was terrified to be without them—and pondered her next
      move.

The relevant predicate in (11) is *be without them,* and the larger context makes it clear that the referent of the understood subject—named Bream—is not volitionally involved in being without them, that is, without the drops for her eyes. The predicate is thus [−Choice].

It was noted above that a passive lower predicate is prototypically associated with a [−Choice] interpretation. It is of interest to probe this context further in the dataset from COCA because the Choice Principle predicts that this environment is congenial to *of -ing* complements. The expectation is borne out in a striking fashion. It turns out that (9b) is the only instance of a *to* infinitive complement in this environment in the dataset and that there are as many as 34 tokens of *of -ing* complements with passive lower clauses. Two examples are given in (12a–b).

(12) a. He is not a strong person and he's terrified of being locked up for a   (2015,
          crime he didn't commit.   FIC)
      b. We were all terrified of being left behind, ...   (2008,
                                                                                   FIC)

To infinitive variants are conceivable for the sentences in (12a–b), as in *We were all terrified to be left behind.* As in the case of complement constructions with the adjective *scared*, the *of -ing* complements are Source-like, with the adjective preserving its basic meaning of "in a state of intense fear." For their part, the *to* infinitive variants are more Goal like, suggesting an imminent event, with the adjective taking on a slightly more abstract sense, conveying a touch of not wanting.

On the other hand, stance-like interpretations of sentential complements where the adjective takes on a more abstract meaning, analogous to those found with the adjectives *afraid* (Rudanko 2015) and *scared* (Chap. 2 of the present volume), are hard to find with *terrified*, as tokens of "not terrified," followed by a *to* infinitive or an *of -ing* complement are far less common in the dataset from COHA and COCA. Two such tokens are found, however; one from each corpus. These two tokens are given in (13a–b).

(13) a. I went methodically through the preflight checklist. Three times. I   (COHA,
began to panic again. Then I realized that I was not really terrified of   1994,
taking off. Nor did flying the pattern—a rectangle around the   FIC)
airport—present any problems.

b. Most of the things he makes his living worrying about have probably   (COCA,
never bothered you, either. You're not, in all likelihood, terrified of   2008,
being killed by your TV. You've probably realized your child's Easy   NEWS)
Bake is unlikely to burn down your house,...

Stance-like interpretations are linked to *to* infinitive complements in Rudanko (2015, 47) and in Chap. 2, and it may be that the preponderance of the *of -ing* complement with *terrified* has inhibited the rise of stance marker-like interpretations. Another possibility is that the basic meaning of *terrified*, "very frightened" in the *OALD* gloss cited above, with its implication of a high degree of fright or fear, may be a factor inhibiting the growth of stance like readings. The question will deserve further investigation.

3.4   *To* INFINITIVE AND *OF -ING* COMPLEMENTS
OF THE ADJECTIVE *TERRIFIED* IN THE BNC

This section turns the focus onto the state of affairs with the two complements of *terrified* in recent British English, using data from the BNC, the British National Corpus, and comparing the results with the results from the corresponding period of COHA, that is, the 1970s, 1980s, and 1990s.[4] As with *scared*, the aim here is to determine whether the British English data on *terrified* indicate similar levels of applicability of the Extraction Principle and the Choice Principle, and, of course, whether the *of-ing* complement is in a similarly dominant position over its rival *to* infinitive with *terrified* in this variety as it is in American English, where it was seen to have gained ground with some efficiency in recent decades.

In response to the search strings "terrified to _V*I" and "terrified of _V*G" the BNC gives a total of 37 tokens for the *to* infinitive, and 58 of the *of-ing* complement.[5] As in the American English data, indirect complements are very frequent among the BNC data, comprising 16 of the total 37 *to* infinitive tokens; the reader is referred back to (3a–b) for examples of this type of pattern. Supplementary searches for relevant tokens with words intervening between the elements of the original search string were carried out, and an additional four tokens were added to the total, all variants of the *of-ing* type. (14a–b) give illustrations.

(14) a.   …she felt unable to study them in detail, so terrified was she of   (ANR
           slipping on the highly polished parquet.   685)
      b.   …terrified of unknowingly swallowing horsemeat in restaurants,   (B34
           many preferred to suffer cold rice pudding at the Club.   1319)

One example of extraction found in the *of-ing* data attests to the inapplicability of the Extraction Principle to the discussion, and this token, along with the indirect complements of the *to* infinitive dataset, was set aside. The total numbers of relevant tokens of *to* infinitive and *of-ing* complements in the BNC are 21 and 61 respectively.

A general and rather obvious point to make when looking at the numbers from the BNC alongside those of 1970–1990s COHA is that the *of-ing* complement is noticeably more prolific than the *to* infinitive competitor also in British English. (The numbers for the relevant decades of COHA are 18 *to* infinitives and 26 *of-ing* complements.) The question of whether one variety of English saw the expansion of the gerundial complement before the other cannot be addressed here on the basis of these limited numbers, but it is an interesting point, and one which invites further attention. The fact that the *of-ing* variant is well ahead of the *to* infinitive in both varieties is a compelling result in itself, and worth noting in view of earlier work (Rudanko 2017, 46; this volume), where the *to* infinitive was seen to be the more frequent of the two patterns even in

Table 3.4 [+Choice] and [−Choice] complements of the adjective *terrified* in the BNC

	[+Choice]	*[−Choice]*	*Total*
to infinitives	19	2	21
of-*ing* complements	21	40	61

recent English. The variation between the two patterns naturally deserves further investigation in the case of other matrix adjectives.

With extraction environments having proved uncommon, the remaining factor to be tested is the Choice Principle. The results of its application to the British English data are shown in Table 3.4.

The results of the Chi square test put the Chi square number at 17.46, meaning that the Choice Principle in this case has a highly significant effect, at $p < 0.0001$ (df = 1).

Examples of [+Choice] and [−Choice] tokens with both complement types in British English are given in (15a–b) and (16a–b) below.

(15) a. Linda had said that she was terrified [pause] to get Lego for the little boy. (KB3 830)

   b. If it was the hospital, she realized she was terrified to hear the news. (JY3 3507)

(16) a. SUEDE singing star Brett Anderson is terrified of going to a rave in case he gets beaten up. (CH1 8918)

   b. ... the King always has to have his own way, and is terrified of being laughed at. (CJR 648)

(15a) and (16a) are both [+Choice] lower predicates, and the reasons given above regarding volitional involvement in, control of, and responsibility for the lower clause action also obtain here. (15b) and (16b), on the other hand, are both [−Choice] environments. As for the prediction that passives will be found with higher frequency in [−Choice] contexts, it is borne out by the BNC data: 10 passives are found here, and all are of the *of*-*ing* [−Choice] type.

A comparison to the significance level obtained for the COHA data from the last three decades of the twentieth century—with the relevant numbers taken from Table 3.2—reveals that the distribution of the two competing variants over that period in American English does not reach the level of statistical significance, a finding which naturally needs confirmation from a larger dataset. On the other hand, the highly significant results of the BNC data allow speculation that the effects of the Choice Principle were more clearly manifest in British English in that period—the low proportion of *to* infinitives in [−Choice] contexts is particularly interesting in this regard.

3.5   CONCLUDING OBSERVATIONS

This chapter looks into the distribution of the *to* infinitive and *of -ing* complements of the adjective *terrified* from the 1840s to the mid-2010s in American English, and the late twentieth century in British English. Data from COHA was supplemented with data from COCA, and comparison was made with British English using material from the BNC. In-depth examination was restricted to the period 1950 to 2015, as very few instances of non-finite complements of any kind are evident in the nineteenth century COHA data; the *of -ing* complement does not appear at all until the 1930s, and the *to* infinitive makes only sporadic appearances throughout the 90 years prior to 1930. From the 1950s onwards, both complements are found in each decade in the COHA data, and both thrive as we approach the more recent decades.

The distribution of the complements of *terrified* is shown to fall very much within the parameters of the Great Complement Shift, in that the gerundial option has gained ground in recent decades, and, according to the data, has in fact outstripped its infinitival competitor in a way that is even somewhat uncharacteristic of this type of complement distribution. It was suggested that the infrequent use of *terrified* with negation and its subsequent inability to act as a stance marker permitting the matrix adjective to take on a more abstract meaning may be a possible factor to have had an effect on the lack of progress made by the *to* infinitive, the complement most clearly linked to the expression of stance with a more abstract interpretation. It was also noted that the *to* infinitive complement is not currently recognized as an option for *terrified* in some standard dictionaries.

The Choice Principle is shown to have a significant effect on complement selection in all three datasets of *terrified*, with highly significant results in a Chi Square test in all cases. As was the case with *scared*, the *to* infinitive is the complement most closely linked to a [+Choice] context, and the *of -ing* complement has the tighter connection to [−Choice] contexts. It was suggested that the *to* infinitive may be more closely linked to

[+Choice] environments in British English, compared to American English, something that would have to be confirmed by further research.

NOTES

1. As was noted in Sect. 3.1, the adjective *terrified* also selects *of* NP complements, and a comment may be appended here on such complements during the period when the sentential *of -ing* pattern was emerging. In Chap. 2 it was observed that in the case of *scared*, *of* NP complements were found to be quite frequent at the time when the sentential pattern was emerging with that adjective, but in the case of *terrified*, the number of such non-sentential complements is much lower in the decades when the sentential pattern was establishing itself. Only one *of* NP complement was found in the 1920s, and only seven in the 1930s, with a normalized frequency of 0.28 for the 1930s. The frequency does rise in the 1940s, with 13 tokens and a frequency of 0.53, and even more in the 1950s, with 18 tokens and a frequency of 0.73. The non-sentential pattern is thus more frequent than the sentential pattern in those decades, but the low frequencies of both make it more difficult than in the case of *scared* to argue that the non-sentential pattern might have aided in the spread of the sentential pattern.

2. We are grateful to an anonymous reader, who pointed out that *to* infinitive constructions selected by emotive adjectives such as *terrified* fall into two semantic categories; the prospective type, as seen in (5a), and the retrospective type, as seen in (5b). A comment on the distinction is given in note 3, on the basis of the more numerous tokens of *to* infinitives in COCA.

3. Regarding the semantic distinction between the prospective and retrospective *to* infinitives, mentioned in the previous note, it appears that while some retrospective *to* infinitives are found, as for instance with the verb *see* in ... *she was terrified to see the results on the screen* (2013, NEWS), most *to* infinitives are of the prospective type, as in *She was terrified to go to school* (2014, NEWS). As a side note, it may be added that the verb *go*, with eight tokens, is the most frequent verb in *to* infinitive complements of the adjective *terrified* in COCA.

4. As was noted in Chap. 2, the make-up of the BNC does not match that of COHA perfectly, for instance with respect to text type. However, both are large corpora with material from different text types, and a comparison seems possible for the purpose of tracking broad historical trends.

5. Because the number of tokens of *terrified* tends to be rather low, with this adjective both the BNCweb CQP edition and the BYU-BNC were searched in order to turn up as many tokens as possible. (It was noticed that sometimes one edition may miss a token, while the other may recognize it.) The search strings given in the text are for the BNCweb CQP edition. The BYU-BNC search strings are the same as were used for COHA.

References

Collins Cobuild Advanced Learner's Dictionary, 8th ed. 2014. Glasgow: HarperCollins Publishers.

Oxford Advanced Learner's Dictionary of Current English, 7th ed. 2005. Oxford: Oxford University Press.

Oxford English Dictionary, 2nd ed. 1989. OED Online. Oxford: Oxford University Press. Accessed February 2017. http://www.oed.com

Rudanko, Juhani. 2015. *Linking Form and Meaning: Studies on Selected Control Patterns in Recent English*. Basingstoke: Palgrave Macmillan.

———. 2017. *Infinitives and Gerunds in Recent English: Studies on Non-Finite Complements with Data from Large Corpora*. London: Palgrave Macmillan Springer.

Semantic Roles and Complement Selection: A Case Study of the Adjective *Afraid*

Abstract Chapter 4 investigates the non-finite complements of the adjective *afraid* in American and British English, using data from selected decades of the Corpus of Historical American English and the British National Corpus. The *to* infinitive and *of -ing* complements are tracked from the 1820s to the 2000s, and the Choice Principle is applied to the corpus data to explain the distribution of the two competing patterns. The notion of affective stance in negative contexts is also considered as a possible factor responsible for the continuing dominance of the *to* infinitive over the *of -ing* complement with *afraid*—a development at odds with the general principles of the Great Complement Shift.

Keywords Subject control • Choice Principle • COHA • BNC

4.1 INTRODUCTION

The adjective *afraid* commonly selects *to* infinitive and *of -ing* complements. The sentential status of both of these is here assumed on the basis of earlier discussion. The two types are illustrated by the sentences in (1a–b), which are taken from COHA.

© The Author(s) 2018

P. Rickman, J. Rudanko, *Corpus-Based Studies on Non-Finite Complements in Recent English,*
https://doi.org/10.1007/978-3-319-72989-3_4

(1)   a.   They were afraid to contradict me, ...   (2006, NEWS)
       b.   ... he was afraid of crushing the munchkin.   (2009, FIC)

Sentences (1a–b) involve subject control, since *afraid* as the higher predicate assigns a semantic role to the higher subject. As in earlier chapters, it is assumed that in current English infinitival *to* is under the Aux node, which is supported by the well-formedness of sentences of the type *They are afraid to contradict me, but some others were not afraid to*. As for *of*, it is of course a preposition. The sentences in (1a–b) may then be represented as in (1a'–b').

(1)   a'.   [[they]$_{NP}$ were [[afraid]$_{Adj}$ [[PRO]$_{NP}$ [to]$_{Aux}$ contradict me]$_{S2}$]$_{AdjP}$]$_{S1}$
       b'.   [[he]$_{NP}$ was [[afraid]$_{Adj}$ [of]$_{Prep}$ [[[PRO]$_{NP}$ crushing the munchkin]$_{S2}$]$_{NP}$]$_{AdjP}$]$_{S1}$

The purpose of this chapter is to investigate and to compare the non-finite complement patterns selected by the adjective *afraid*. Information is gathered on the incidence of the two types of complements in recent English, and as in Chaps. 2 and 3 of this book, particular attention is paid to the possible relevance of the Choice Principle as a factor to explain variation between the two alternants. This question was examined in Rudanko (2015, Chap. 3) on the basis of three consecutive decades of the *TIME* Corpus, the 1920s, the 1930s, and the 1940s, and it was concluded that the principle was a salient factor bearing on the variation in question in those decades. The present study investigates a different dataset with data from COHA. The adjective *afraid* is quite frequent in English, especially with *to* infinitives, and for practical reasons, COHA is not investigated in its entirety. Instead, the focus is placed on three decades of the corpus. The most recent decade, the 2000s, was chosen in order to gain information on current usage, and it is also of interest to gain a historical perspective and for this reason the 1820s was chosen. (While the 1810s is the earliest decade covered by COHA, it would have been a less suitable choice because the subcorpus for that decade is rather small.) To supplement the data from the early and late parts of COHA, data from a third decade was also included, and the choice of the 1910s for this purpose seemed appropriate, since it is smack in the middle.

As regards commentary in dictionaries on comparing *to* infinitive and *of* -*ing* complements of the adjective *afraid*, it is easy enough to find accounts indicating or implying that the two are close in meaning. This is the gist of the glosses and comments in the account in the *OED* reviewed in Rudanko (2015, 225–226), and these are taken for granted here. They may be supplemented with a reference to the analysis of the adjective and its patterns of complementation in the 7th edition of the *OALD* (2005). The dictionary identifies three senses, and for the first two of them *to* infinitive and *of*-*ing* complements are cited side by side as being among the possible constructions with the sense in question. The first sense is "feeling fear; frightened because you think that you might be hurt or suffer," as in *She was afraid to open the door and I started to feel afraid of going out at night OALD*, s.v.). The second sense is "worried about what might happen," as in *Don't be afraid to ask if you don't understand* and *She was afraid of upsetting her parents.* (*OALD*, s.v.). The analysis in the *OALD* citing both constructions under both senses again shows that they are close in meaning. The semantic similarity of the two constructions makes the task of separating them, in the spirit of Bolinger's Generalization, all the more challenging, but also all the more intriguing.

4.2   The Choice Principle in Three Decades of COHA

Turning to the analysis of data from the three decades selected from COHA, it seems appropriate to proceed chronologically, beginning with the 1820s. The adjective *afraid* is quite common with *to* infinitives, and fairly common with *of*-*ing* complements, and the search string "afraid to [v?i*]" suggests itself for the *to* infinitives and the search string "afraid of [v?g*]" suggests itself for *of*-*ing* complements.[1] The number of *to* infinitives retrieved from the 1820s is 151 and the corresponding number of *of* -*ing* complements is 44. The size of the subcorpus for the 1820s is 6.9 million words, and the normalized frequencies are 21.9 per million for *to* infinitives and 6.4 per million for *of*-*ing* complements. Initial examples of the two types from the 1820s are given in (2a–b).

(2) a.   Harold was anxious, yet afraid to touch her hand.   (1822, FIC)
     b.   I was afraid of familiarizing her to such things, ...   (1823, FIC)

There are no indirect complements among the 195 tokens. As regards extractions, there are only three of them. An example is given in (3).

(3) … in such a body of men, and thus situated, we should not be afraid to   (1828,
      repose absolute legislative power, so far, at least, as is necessary to regulate   MAG)
      the common transactions between man and man.

All three extractions are out of *to* infinitive complements in the present dataset and there are no extractions out of *of -ing* complements, which is in accordance with the Extraction Principle. Taking the well-established status of the Extraction Principle into account, the three tokens are set aside here. This leaves 148 *to* infinitives and 44 *of -ing* complements to be considered.

Proceeding to the [+/−Choice] distinction as a possible factor bearing on the variation between the two alternants in the present dataset, the same criteria can be used as were applied in Chaps. 2 and 3. The results of the analysis are given in Table 4.1.

Applying the Chi Square test to the numbers in Table 4.1, the Chi Square obtained is as high as 58.79, and the results are significant at the level of $p < 0.0001$ (df = 1).

Illustrations from the present data set are given in (4a–b) and (5a–b).

(4) a. I turned away, immediately. I was afraid to look any longer.   (1823,
                                                                          FIC)
      b. The arts of peace are beneficent and gentle. Those of war, tumultuous   (1823,
          and confounding. "Nay,—(after a pause during which he uncovered his   FIC)
          bald head—and lifted up his large, full eyes to the sky, as if he were
          overheard there—and was not ashamed, nor afraid to be overheard
          there) … "
(5) a. … lest this should destroy the freedom of debate, and make the   (1828,
          Members afraid of speaking their thoughts with honesty and plainness   NF)
          in matters for the public good.
      b. … they were so dirty that she was afraid of contracting some infectious   (1828,
          disorder.   FIC)

Table 4.1 [+Choice] and [−Choice] complements of the adjective *afraid* in the 1820s

	[+Choice]	[−Choice]	Total
to infinitives	137	11	148
of -ing	17	27	44

The lower predicates in (4a) and (5a) are *look any longer* and *speaking their thoughts with honesty and plainness in matters for the public good*. Both of these encode a conceptualization of an action or event such that the referent of the understood subject is volitionally involved in it, has control over it and can be held responsible for it. Both predicates are therefore [+Choice]. By contrast, the contexts *be overheard there* and *contracting some infectious disorder*, as used in (4b) and (5b), conceptualize an event that the referent of the understood subject is neither volitionally involved in, nor in control of, nor responsible for, and the contexts are [−Choice].

The lower predicate in (4b) is a passive, which is a prototypical [−Choice] environment. In view of the overall salience of the Choice Principle as a factor explaining variation in the present dataset, the expectation is that in general such environments would favor the *of-ing* complement. This expectation is borne out, for it turns out that (4b) is the only token where a *to* infinitive occurs with a passive lower clause. By contrast, there are as many as 15 tokens where an *of-ing* complement is found with a passive lower clause. Two examples of this combination are given in (6a–b).

(6) a.   ... I was not afraid of being obstructed or bewildered.   (1827, FIC)
     b.   They are afraid of being considered tame characters.   (1829, NF)

The preponderance of *of-ing* complements in the environment of passive lower clauses is predicted by the Choice Principle.

Turning to the 1910s, the size of the subcorpus for that decade is 22.7 million words, and the search strings retrieve 376 *to* infinitive complements and 87 *of-ing* complements. Among the 376 *to* infinitives retrieved by the search string there is one token where the *to* infinitive is an indirect complement. This is given in (7).

(7) Link is on the watch to do harm, the girls will be almost too afraid to   (1910,
     go out-   FIC)

The indirect complement can be excluded from further consideration. This leaves us with 375 *to* infinitives and 87 *of-ing* complements. The normalized frequency is thus 16.5 per million words for *to* infinitives, and the corresponding frequency is 3.8 per million for *of-ing* complements. Both constructions have therefore become less frequent, and the decrease is especially noticeable in the case of the *of-ing* complement, from 6.4 per million words to 3.8 per million words. This finding is not in the spirit of the Great Complement Shift, and it deserves to be noted.

As far as extractions in the sense of the Extraction Principle are concerned, they are rare in the dataset and only seven are found. Two illustrations are given in (8a–b).

(8) a. Someone told me once that to do something you were really afraid   (1914,
         to do was really the bravest thing …   FIC)
     b. Is there anything about you and your life here that you'd be afraid to (1916,
         tell me?   FIC)

In all seven tokens with extraction, the complement is a *to* infinitive, as is the case in (8a–b). Given the well-established status of the Extraction Principle, the seven tokens are set aside here.

The next step is to consider the remaining 368 *to* infinitives and the 87 *of*-*ing* complements from the point of view of the Choice Principle. Table 4.2 gives information on the numbers of [+Choice] and [−Choice] lower clauses in relation to *to* infinitive and *of*-*ing* complements in the present dataset.

The Chi Square is as high as 186.44, and the results are significant at the level of $p < 0.0001$ (df = 1).

Illustrations of [+Choice] and [−Choice] lower predicates are given in (9a–b) and (10a–b).

(9)   a. He was afraid to make a speech.   (1912,
                                                                             FIC)
      b. He is never afraid to see men of tried honesty and high principles (1912,
          nominated for office.   MAG)
(10) a. For Dexter had no need to be afraid of walking the streets of   (1911,
          Gridley.   FIC)
      b. I shake all over. I'm afraid of going nuts.   (1919,
                                                                             MAG)

Table 4.2 [+Choice] and [−Choice] complements of the adjective *afraid* in the 1910s

	[+Choice]	*[−Choice]*	*Total*
to infinitives	345	23	368
of-*ing*	26	61	87

The lower clauses in (9a) and (10a) are [+Choice], and those in (9b) and (10b) are [−Choice]. For instance, the lower predicate in (10b) is *going nuts*, and it conveys that the referent of the understood subject was neither volitionally involved in (the process of) going nuts, nor in control of it, nor responsible for it. As for *see* in (9b), it is experiential and nonagentive (cf. Gruber 1967). This is not to say that *see* cannot have agentive and [+Choice] uses or senses. In the present dataset an agentive use occurs in (11).

(11)   He was first taken sick with pains in the legs, hands and arms, and went   (1914,
       to morning sick call, but could never get anything done because he was a   NF)
       little deaf, and could not hear what the doctor said and so could explain
       no further, and he was in a very bad fix. They did nothing for him and he
       was afraid to see the doctor, because he would have been impatient, and
       would have sent him to the hole, and then he would lose time.

In (11) the predicate *see the doctor* appears to have the sense "consult the doctor," and it is among the [+Choice] tokens.

The presence of passive lower clauses in the 1910s dataset—and their role in relation to the Choice Principle—shows a similar picture to that obtained from the 1820s dataset, with passives occurring more frequently with the *of-ing* complement than the *to* infinitive. Likewise, in accordance with the expected distribution, all passives are linked with a [−Choice] environment. Examples are given in (12a–b).

(12)   a.   OLD-man didn't care much if the Wolf did drown. He was afraid to   (1915,
            be left alone and hungry in the snow—that was all.   NF)
       b.   Annie and Lou sometimes speak Swedish at home, but Annie is   (1913,
            almost as much afraid of being "caught" at it as ever her mother   FIC)
            was of being caught barefoot.

In the present dataset, passive lower clauses account for two of the 368 *to* infinitive tokens, and 21 of the 87 *of-ing* complements.

Proceeding to the 2000s, the most recent full decade of COHA, the size of the subcorpus is 29.6 million words, and the search strings retrieve 448 *to* infinitive complements. As for *of-ing* complements, the total number of tokens retrieved is 117. Among the 448 *to* infinitives there are as many as 18 indirect complements, all of them featuring the word *too* as a premodifier of the adjective. From this it appears that indirect complements have become considerably more frequent in recent times. Two examples are given in (13a–b).

(13) a.   But the people who don't like Kurt are too afraid to say anything,   (2005,
           because Kurt is the president of the senior class ...   FIC)
      b.   I was too afraid to stand or even sit up.   (2003,
                                                                                  FIC)

When the 18 tokens of indirect complements are set aside, there remain 430 *to* infinitive and 117 *of*-*ing* complements of the adjective. The normalized frequencies are 14.5 per million words for *to* infinitives and 3.5 per million words for *of*-*ing* complements. Both types of complements therefore continue to be relatively frequent with the adjective *afraid*, but when the findings for the 2000s are compared with the corresponding frequencies for the 1910s, the present study suggests that both *to* infinitives and *of*-*ing* complements have become slightly less frequent in current English. What is of greater theoretical interest is that as far as the adjective *afraid* is concerned, the *to* infinitive complement has maintained its clear predominance over the *of*-*ing* complement even in the most recent full decade. This finding again runs counter to the spirit of the Great Complement Shift, and deserves to be noted (see Sect. 4.3).

Turning to the factors that may bear on the choice between the two types of sentential complements in the dataset for the 2000s, the Extraction Principle is relevant to 14 tokens. In 12 of these the complement is a *to* infinitive and in two the complement is of the *of*-*ing* type. Two illustrations are given in (14a–b).

(14) a.   ... got to think about the playoffs, and it's not a goal we're   (2005,
           afraid to talk about.   NEWS)
      b.   She was like a glass he was afraid of dropping.   (2007, FIC)

In both (14a) and (14b) the extraction rule is Relativization. The overwhelming predominance of *to* infinitives in extraction contexts is in the spirit of the Extraction Principle and taking into account the well-established status of the Extraction Principle, the 14 tokens can be set aside from further consideration.

With extractions set aside, there remain 418 *to* infinitives and 115 *of*-*ing* complements to be considered in relation to the Choice Principle. Table 4.3 gives information on the numbers of [+Choice] and [−Choice] lower predicates among the two types of complements.

Table 4.3 [+Choice] and [−Choice] complements of the adjective *afraid* in the 2000s

	[+Choice]	*[−Choice]*	*Total*
to infinitives	378	40	418
of -*ing*	37	78	115

The Chi Square here is as high as 174.20, and the results are significant at the level of $p < 0.0001$ (df = 1).

Illustrations of [+Choice] and [−Choice] contexts are given in (15a–b) and (16a–b).

(15) a. He was a genius, not afraid to make the bold move. (2007, NEWS)

   b. The qadi of Aden, afraid to lose his income from his constituency, raised objections. (2004, NF)

(16) a. Sure, Neil stuck to the Spartan way of life while Yves wasn't afraid of taking advantage of his privileged pupils. (2003, MAG)

   b. There were a few more letters, cryptic or guarded, as if Grace was afraid of having them read by anyone else. (2007, FIC)

The predicates *make the bold move* and *taking advantage of his privileged pupils*, as used in (15a) and (16a), are [+Choice], encoding an event or action that the referent of the subject is volitionally involved in, has control over, and is responsible for. By contrast, the predicates *lose his income from his constituency* and *having them read by anyone else*, as used in (15b) and (16b) are [−Choice]. They conceptualize an event as happening to the referent of the lower subject. For instance, in (16b) the construction consisting of the string *"have* NP past participle" has a happenstance interpretation, reporting what may happen to a person, which is non-causative in nature and [−Choice] (Rudanko 2012, 231).

In light of the evidence of Tables 4.1, 4.2 and 4.3 it seems clear that the Choice Principle is a factor that has an impact on complement selection of the adjective *afraid*. It is worth probing this finding further by considering lower predicates in the passive. This is a [−Choice] environment par excellence, and in view of the Choice Principle the expectation is that this environment might be hospitable to *of* -*ing* complements. There are 36 tokens with passive lower clauses in the data for the 2000s, and of these eight are *to* infinitives and 26 are *of* -*ing* complements. There is thus indeed a striking preponderance of *of -ing* complements in this environment. Two illustrations of each type are given in (17a–b) and (18a–b).

(17) a. … ran up the stairs ahead of her, as if afraid to be left behind   (2004, FIC)
          among them.
      b. Ruth, Mary, and Penny ordered barbeque sandwiches and   (2000, FIC)
          Brunswick stew, and kept their sunglasses on, as if afraid to be
          recognized.
(18) a. Not sure what you want? Afraid of getting ripped off?   (2003,
                                                                              MAG)
      b. Hollywood producers have entered the new fray because they're   (2003,
          afraid of being frozen out if network clout grows.   NEWS)

Almost all the passive lower clauses are of the normal *be -en* type, as in (17a–b) and (18b), but there is also the odd token of a *get* passive, as in (18a).

It is not always easy to separate the patterns in sentences of the type of (17a–b) and (18a–b), but it is desirable to offer a comment, in the spirit of Bolinger's Generalization. The difference is subtle, but the Goal-like nature of *to* infinitives suggests an imminent event about to happen, and it may also convey some element of volitional involvement on the part of the referent of the understood subject. By contrast, with a gerundial complement the adjective retains its basic meaning "in a state of fear" more fully, with the complement expressing the source of fear.

4.3   FURTHER DISCUSSION OF THE FINDINGS

The investigation of the complement selection properties of the adjective *afraid* in the 1820s, 1910s and 2000s yields a number of noteworthy results. Most important from the point of view of the Choice Principle is the finding, clear from Tables 4.1, 4.2, and 4.3, that in each of the three decades the principle was confirmed as a significant factor bearing on the complement choices of the adjective. It is also observed that the Chi Squares calculated for each decade are quite high, and that they are especially high for the two later decades when the number of tokens is higher.

In addition to the major finding about the salience of the Choice Principle, it was also observed that *to* infinitive complements continue to be very frequent with the adjective. There is a slight overall downward trend in the normalized frequencies of *to* infinitive complements; for instance, from the 1910s to the 2000s the frequency goes down from 16.5 to 14.5 per million words. However, there is also a slight overall downward trend in the frequency of the *of-ing* construction; from the 1910s to the 2000s it goes down from 3.8 to 3.5 per million words. What is most striking is that even in the most recent decade the *to* infinitive is several times more frequent with the adjective than the *of-ing* complement. This finding runs counter to the spirit of the Great Complement Shift, and this finding also deserves some further comment.

One simple factor in play may be that the "*afraid to* Verb..." construction is frequent, and linguistic change may happen more slowly—or may fail to happen at all—with a high frequency construction. In addition to this general principle, it may be possible to consider other factors. One may be related to the Choice Principle. It is noteworthy that in each of the decades considered large pluralities of *to* infinitives are [+Choice] and large pluralities of gerundial complements are [−Choice]. The semantic specialization of each type of construction may thus have protected the *to* infinitive and rendered it less vulnerable to encroachment by the *of-ing* pattern.

Another factor that is worth bringing up relates to the pragmatic and interactional interpretation of each type of construction from the point of view of the notion of stance (see also Rudanko 2015, 37–38). Stance has been taken to relate to the "linguistic means by which speakers and writers convey their personal attitudes and emotions, their evaluations and assessments, and their level of commitment towards propositions" (Gray and Biber 2014, 219). For instance, consider sentence (19), from Gray and Biber (2014, 221).

(19) I was afraid to travel alone, I guess.

Sentence (19) is an illustration of how the "head of the matrix clause/phrase is a controlling word that conveys a particular stance meaning relative to the proposition expressed by the complement clause" (Gray and Biber 2014, 221). Sentence (19) has a first person subject, and stance is explicitly attributed to the speaker/writer. With a third person subject, this is "less explicit," as in *He hopes to start Saturday,* and such "structures are sometimes omitted from stance analyses" (Gray and Biber 2014, 222). Here we have decided to consider a broader view of stance than is "sometimes" done, and we also pay heed to less explicit structures, to explore the role of stance in complement selection more fully.

Expressions of stance may be analyzed on the basis of the categories of evidentiality or "epistemic stance," relating to knowledge (often certainty or doubt), affect or "attitudinal stance," relating to feelings and attitudes, and "style of speaking stance," relating to "comments on the communication itself" (Biber et al. 1999, 972–975). The stance expressed by *afraid* with its complement in (19) is clearly of the affect type, conveying an emotion—that of fear—relative to the content of the following *to* infinitive. In their discussion of complement types in this connection, Gray and Biber (2014, 221) focus on *to* infinitives and *that* clauses selected by adjectives, nouns and verbs, and Biber et al. (1999, 974–975) also illustrate an *of -ing* complement selected by a noun, but it seems to the present investigators that a particular stance meaning—that of fear—can also be discerned in the case of an *of -ing* complement selected by the adjective *afraid*, as in (20).

(20)   I was afraid of turning around and meeting her gaze.   (2005, FIC)

The combination of a stance adjective with a following *to* infinitive complement has been recognized as a stance construction (Gray and Biber 2014, 228), but the present study suggests that the combination of a stance adjective with a following *of -ing* complement may also be included in the inventory of stance constructions in English.

At a more delicate level, it may be possible to use the notion of affective stance to assist in the often difficult task of separating the two types of sentential complement. This concerns the construction where the head adjective is negated. *Not* is the most frequent and the most prototypical negative word in English, but it is of course not the only negative that can negate the predication of the adjective *afraid*. Consider the examples of *to* infinitive complements in (21a–c), all taken from the most recent decade.

(21) a.   Well, let me tell you. I am not afraid to be controversial or to   (2000, FIC)
            speak my mind, ...
      b.   Victor may be a lot of things, but at least he's not afraid to fight   (2005, FIC)
            for what he wants.
      c.   I wanted a modern-day personification of knightliness, Ceej, a   (2005, FIC)
            man who's not afraid to laugh triumphantly in the face of death.

There are 134 tokens where the predication of *afraid* is negated among the 418 relevant tokens of *to* infinitives for the 2000s, representing 32.1 per cent of the total. The examples in (21a–c) are from among them, and in these examples the construction in question takes on a sense that goes beyond a simple sense of "not in a state of fear (relative to the proposition expressed by the lower clause)." In these sentences the construction suggests a stance of defiance in the face of potential or perceived opposition or difficulty,[2] a stance which may be termed "reactive" or "assertive." As for the sense of *not afraid* in (21a–c), it approaches that of *be prepared/ ready (to do sth)*, and carries less of the basic sense of *be not in fear (of sth)*.

Cues may often be found in the context that can trigger or strengthen the interactional interpretation of defiance that may be carried by the "not afraid to Verb ..." construction. The cues often concern the nature of the lower predicate, and for instance the predicates *be controversial or to speak my mind* in (21a) and *fight for what he wants* in (21b) suggest defiance and confrontation. Or the effect of defiance may be encoded by phrases such as *triumphantly in the face of death*, as in (21c). Not all tokens of "not afraid to Verb ..." construction involve an interactional stance of defiance in the face of opposition or difficulty, but many do, and such an assertive or reactive stance seems less likely with the *of -ing* complement.[3] In this connection, it may also be pointed out that among the 115 tokens of relevant *of -ing* complements in the most recent decade, there are only 21 tokens where *afraid* is negated, which represents 18.3 per cent of the total, and is a considerably lower proportion than the corresponding proportion in the case of *to* infinitive complements. Overall, then, the semantic and pragmatic flexibility of the *to* infinitive complement is one factor that may explain, at least in part, why the pattern has been, and is, able to maintain its predominance over the gerundial pattern even in very recent English.

4.4   *To* Infinitive and *of -ing* Complements of the Adjective *Afraid* in the BNC

This section turns to an investigation of the *to* infinitive and *of -ing* patterns involving subject control in the BNC, the British National Corpus, in relation to the findings of the previous section. The BNC is not the perfect corpus to be investigated in conjunction with COHA, for instance because of differences in the text types featured in these corpora. However, what recommends it for present purposes is its size and variety of text types. At the same time, it should be borne in mind that the corpus represents slightly older usage in comparison with the decade of the 2000s of COHA.

The discussion and the findings of Sect. 4.2 can be taken for granted as a point of departure for the present section, and the major purpose is to determine if the Choice Principle is as relevant to the analysis of British English as it was found to be to the American English data in Sect. 4.2. A further goal is to find out if the predominance of the *to* infinitive pattern in relation to the *of -ing* pattern is as overwhelming in British English as it was found to be in American English.

The search strings, using the CQP-edition of the BNCweb, are "afraid to _V*I" and "afraid of _V*G" for the *to* infinitive and the *of -ing* complements respectively. They yield 664 tokens of the former and 217 of the latter. Among the *to* infinitives there are two duplicates, which are counted only once, reducing the total to 662. Among the 662 tokens there are 29 indirect complements. Two illustrations are given in (22a–b). (Unless otherwise noted, all examples in this section are from the BNC.)

(22) a. She just completely lost her nerve and was too afraid to tell him   (JY4
         for fear of rejection.   4164)
     b. … many people are living in fear, often too afraid to go out at   (K55
         night.   6297)

Indirect complements deserve to be noted, but they can be set aside, since this study concerns complements selected by the adjective *afraid*. With the 29 indirect complements set aside, there remain 633 *to* infinitive and 217 *of -ing* complements. The normalized frequency of *to* infinitives is thus 6.3 per million words, and that of *of -ing* complements is 2.2 per million words. Both of these normalized frequencies are lower than the corresponding frequencies in the 2000s in COHA given in Sect. 4.2, and in the case of the *to* infinitive complement the difference is striking. In light of the present data, the construction appears to be much more frequent in the American English corpus. Clearly, this finding is an invitation for more work on the frequency of the construction in British English. At the same time, the general finding that *to* infinitive complements are much more frequent than *of -ing* complements of the adjective, observed for American English in Sect. 4.2, also holds for the BNC data.

Regarding extractions among the 633 *to* infinitives and 217 *of -ing* complements, there are 10 extractions among the former and three among the latter. This is broadly in accordance with the Extraction Principle. Two examples of each are given in (23a–b) and (24a–b).

(23) a. ... there is rage beneath the sunny smile, anger which sufferers are afraid to express. (ECM 1401)

b. ... answers to the questions you always wanted to know but were afraid to ask. (K6A 9)

(24) a. Look, what are you afraid of saying? (H9T 102)

b. You know what we're afraid of saying in case they hear us. (HP1 671)

Given the established status of the Extraction Principle, the 13 tokens are set aside. This leaves 623 *to* infinitives and 214 *of*-*ing* complements to be considered with respect to the Choice Principle.

The tokens in (25a–b) and (26a–b) illustrate the application of the Choice Principle to the data in the BNC.

(25) a. She had been afraid to tell Nancy's story to Dr Losberne, ... (FRK 1661)

b. ... Alida could surely manage, surely was not afraid to be left alone? (AD1 2749)

(26) a. We can still be afraid of expressing our anger, unable to vent our rage. (B21 215)

b. Many family arguments are made worse because people are afraid of losing their dignity. (ALH 1111)

(25a) and (26a) illustrate [+Choice] lower predicates, conveying that the referents of their understood subjects are volitionally involved in the actions in question, have control over them and are responsible for them. By contrast, the predicates *be left alone* and *losing their dignity*, as used in (25b) and (26b), are [−Choice]. (25b) represents a prototypical [−Choice] context, with a passive lower clause. The illustrations in (25b) and (26a) also show that the Choice Principle cannot be a categorical rule in the BNC.

While the Choice Principle is clearly not a categorical rule, it is of interest to investigate whether it represents a statistically significant tendency in the British English data. Table 4.4 gives information on the numbers of [+Choice] and [−Choice] predicates of *to* infinitive and *of*-*ing* complements in the BNC.

The Chi Square is as high as 356.04, and the results are significant at the level of $p < 0.0001$ (df = 1).

The finding that the Choice Principle is statistically significant in the analysis of the British English data provides further confirmation of the

Table 4.4 [+Choice] and [−Choice] complements of the adjective *afraid* in the BNC

	[+Choice]	[−Choice]	Total
to infinitives	589	34	623
of -*ing*	71	143	214

principle, but it is also of interest further to probe the potential salience of the principle in the case of passive lower clauses. Two further illustrations of each type are given in (27a–b) and (28a–b).

(27) a. He was not afraid to be seen deep in conversation with a   (CCL 335)
          Samaritan woman ...
     b. Don't be afraid to be fired.   (C9U 63)
(28) a. European manufacturers are afraid of getting left behind if the   (CSM 70)
          merging handheld personal communicators generate ...
     b. ... girls married in haste and repented at leisure then because   (CEB 1155)
          they were afraid of being left on the shelf.

Virtually all the passives in question are again of the regular *be -en* type, as in (27a–b) and (28b), and *get* passives, as in (28a), are very rare.

Overall, there are as many as 47 tokens where the lower clause is in the passive. In 42 of these the complement is of the *of* -*ing* type, and only in five is it a *to* infinitive. The predominance of the gerundial pattern in the passive environment lends further support to the Choice Principle, taking into account that, overall, *to* infinitives are much more frequent than *of* -*ing* complements in the BNC. As for the *to* infinitive construction in the passive environment, the Goal-like nature of a *to* infinitive may again suggest an imminent event, something that cannot be prevented, as in (27b), which is similar to what was observed in the American English data.

In the discussion of the American English data it was pointed out that a relatively large proportion of *to* infinitival complements, 32.1 per cent, involved negation of the adjective *afraid*, and that as far as the gerundial pattern is concerned, the corresponding proportion was lower, at 18.3 per cent. In the BNC data under review here, the difference between the corresponding proportions is even larger. Among the 623 *to* infinitive complements there are as many as 276 tokens where the adjective *afraid* is negated. This represents a percentage of 44.3 per cent of the total. On the other hand, among the 214 *of-ing* complements of *afraid*, there are only 49 tokens where the predicate *afraid* is negated. This represents a percentage of 22.9 per cent.

It was also noted in the discussion of the American English data how a construction consisting of NEG and a *to* infinitive complement may be linked to an interactional stance of defiance in the face of difficulty or opposition, and how different types of clues may trigger or reinforce such a stance interpretation. In the British English data, there are also numerous tokens that are of interest in this connection. Consider the illustrations in (29a–e).

(29)
a. For the first time in his life he was aware of a blissful inner peace. He was no longer afraid to go home. Father Poole and his prayers had exorcised that particular fear. (B1X 1961)

b. The Loss Adjuster and the branch should not be afraid to challenge the proposed course of remedial work where the Consulting Engineers are recommending ... (HB6 192)

c. On a more serious note, Rowell was a very impressive coach, demanding on the training field, decisively analytical off it—yet not afraid to speak out over indignities such as the Ubogy affair. (CB3 881)

d. "I want more emphasis on the fear of deterrents than the fear of crime," he said. "Unlike the Labour Party we are not afraid to use the P-word—punishment." (KSM 474)

e. Old Eugene had never worked in his life due to what he said was a bad heart, but he never lacked in daring and was never afraid to take a gamble. (ATE 1809)

In (29a) the adjective *afraid* appears to carry its basic sense of "in a state of fear" even with a *to* infinitive, since the co-text makes reference to this emotion in the next sentence. However, less basic interpretations are easily found among *to* infinitives in the context of a negated *afraid*. For instance, this appears to be the case in (29b–e). It is often the nature of the lower predicate that triggers or fosters a defiance interpretation of the construction "NEG *afraid to* VP." Sentence (29b) is a case in point, with its lower predicate *challenge the proposed course of remedial work*. In (29c) the phrase *Unlike the Labour Party* in initial position is another type of clue indicating that a position of one party is being challenged or opposed. Such an interactional stance, where the meaning of *afraid* is at some remove from the basic meaning of the adjective, seems less likely with an *of-ing* complement. With an *of-ing* complement, the adjective retains its basic meaning "in a state of fear" more fully. In this connection, consider the authentic sentence in (30).

(30) I wasn't afraid of losing my boyfriend while I was in prison, because I've   (FR5
      seen people who've been in for two years and their boyfriends still come   1527)
      and visit them.

The key part of the sentence might be paraphrased "I wasn't in a state of fear that I would/might lose my boyfriend while I was in prison," with the "because" clause giving a reason why the person was not in a state of fear. A *to* infinitive complement would not be impossible, setting the "because" clause aside, for *I wasn't afraid to lose my boyfriend while I was in prison* is conceivable, but suggests a meaning along the lines of "I was prepared to lose my boyfriend while I was in prison," where the sense of *afraid* is again at some remove from the basic meaning of the adjective.

4.5   CONCLUDING OBSERVATIONS

This chapter examines *to* infinitive and *of -ing* complements of the central adjective *afraid* in three decades of COHA, the 1820s, 1910s and the 2000s, and the investigation was supplemented with a consideration of fairly recent British English on the basis of the BNC. *To* infinitives were found to be more frequent in each decade of COHA, but fairly large numbers of *of -ing* complements were also encountered. The search strings used also retrieved indirect complements. These are not immediately relevant to the present study, but they turned out to be very rare in the 1820s and in the 1910s, but much more frequent in the 2000s. As for explanatory principles to account for variation among complements of the adjective *afraid*, the Extraction Principle is a well-established generalization, but extractions were found to be relatively rare in all three decades of COHA, and they were also fairly rare in the BNC data. The extractions that did occur tended to involve *to* infinitive complements, which is in accordance with the Extraction Principle.

A major objective of this chapter was to investigate the data of the three decades of COHA from the point of view of the Choice Principle. The principle is not a categorical rule, but it turned out to be highly significant in each of the three decades of COHA, and it was also found to be a significant factor in the case of the BNC data. The application of the principle was supplemented with comments on passive lower clauses both in COHA and the BNC. This environment is prototypically [−Choice], and the Choice Principle therefore predicts that it should be an environment that is favorable to gerundial complements. This expectation was borne out in the decades of COHA considered and in the BNC, thus providing further support for the Choice Principle. At the same time, it was also observed that some exceptions are found, and comments were appended on their interpretation.

One striking finding in this chapter also concerned the continuing predominance of the *to* infinitive pattern in relation to the gerundial construction. This runs counter to the spirit of the Great Complement Shift. A number of possible reasons were suggested that may help explain the failure of the gerundial pattern to gain more traction with the adjective *afraid*. Among them was the suggestion that the pragmatic flexibility of the infinitival pattern entails a versatility that may have helped to maintain the high frequency of the *to* infinitive pattern with the adjective. The proportion of *to* infinitives selected by a negated *afraid* in relation to non-negated *afraid* turned out to be high, especially in the BNC data, and it was suggested that such constructions may function as stance markers signifying a stance of defiance in the face of difficulty or opposition, with *afraid* taking on a meaning that is at some remove from the basic meaning of the adjective.

NOTES

1. While it is quite possible to find examples of words falling between *afraid* and *to/of*, or between *to/of* and the following verb, supplementary searches to capture all such tokens were not carried out in the present chapter. In the authors' opinion, the data obtained from the simple search string alone offers a suitable perspective on the situation, retrieving sufficient numbers of tokens for the purposes of the present study.
2. It may be possible to regard the construction "not afraid to ..." as an "affect key," in the sense of Ochs and Schieffelin (1989) and earlier work. As Ochs and Schieffelin (1989, 15) point out, affect keys may index a range of emotions and attitudes, including "anger, sarcasm, disappointment, sadness, pleasure, humor" and so on. Defiance in the face of difficulty or opposition is not included in their list, but seems a conceivable addition.
3. From a constructional perspective, it may be noted that constructions can be identified at different structural levels of complexity (see de Smet 2008, 65; 2013, 34–35). It then seems possible to say that in the case of the pattern "*not afraid to* Verb," the higher level construction comprising not only the *to* infinitive clause but also the negation and the matrix adjective *afraid* exerts, or may exert, a more pervasive effect on semantic or pragmatic inter-

pretation than what occurs in the case of the "*not afraid of* V-*ing*" construction. In the latter case the lower level constructions—including both the adjective as a construction and the *of -ing* complement as a construction—maintain more of their independence and the higher level construction is less amenable to being interpreted as a reactive stance construction.

The constructional perspective brings to the fore the question of why a reactive interpretation should arise more readily in the case of the *to* infinitive pattern, and not in the case of the *of -ing* pattern. This question will deserve attention. One line of inquiry would be to investigate whether the larger syntactic boundary between the matrix adjective and the clausal complement in the gerundial pattern might be a factor protecting the relative independence of the lower-level construction in the case of the gerundial pattern.

REFERENCES

Biber, Douglas, Stig Johansson, Geoffrey Leech, Susan Conrad, and Edward Finegan. 1999. *Longman Grammar of Spoken and Written English*. London: Longman.

De Smet, Hendrik. 2008. *Diffusional Change in the English System of Complementation. Gerunds, Participles and* for...to *Infinitives*. Doctoral Dissertation, Catholic University of Leuven.

———. 2013. *Spreading Patterns. Diffusional Change in the English System of Complementation*. Oxford: Oxford University Press.

Gray, Bethany, and Douglas Biber. 2014. Stance Markers. In *Corpus Pragmatics: A Handbook*, ed. Karin Aijmer and Christoph Rühlemann, 219–248. Cambridge: Cambridge University Press.

Gruber, Jeffrey S. 1967. Look and See. *Language* 43 (4): 937–947.

Ochs, Elinor, and Bambi B. Schieffelin. 1989. Language has a Heart. *Text* 9: 7–25.

Oxford Advanced Learner's Dictionary of Current English, 7th ed. 2005. Oxford: Oxford University Press.

Rudanko, Juhani. 2012. Exploring Aspects of the Great Complement Shift, with Evidence from the TIME Corpus and COCA. In *The Oxford Handbook of the History of English*, ed. Terttu Nevalainen and Elizabeth Closs Traugott, 222–232. Oxford: Oxford University Press.

———. 2015. *Linking Form and Meaning: Studies on Selected Control Patterns in Recent English*. Basingstoke: Palgrave Macmillan.

Null Objects and Sentential Complements, with Evidence from the Corpus of Historical American English and Hansard

Abstract The present chapter discusses the occurrence of covert NP objects in object control structures with the matrix verb *warn*. The existence of such structures is at odds with Bach's Generalization, which effectively states that the NP object in an object control structure may not be omitted. Evidence from COHA and the Hansard Corpus is introduced and discussed, to shed new light on the apparent exceptions to the Generalization. The frequency of the construction is tracked over the course of the past two centuries in both American and British English, and the nature of the covert NP object is also examined. The question is examined on the basis of corpus data, and the question is also raised as to whether the interpretation of the understood NP might shed light on the use of the covert pattern, understood as a construction in American and British English.

Keywords Understood objects • Bach's Generalization • Object control • Diachronic change • American English • British English

© The Author(s) 2018
P. Rickman, J. Rudanko, *Corpus-Based Studies on Non-Finite Complements in Recent English,*
https://doi.org/10.1007/978-3-319-72989-3_5

5.1   Introduction

Consider sentences (1a–c), from the Corpus of Historical American English, COHA:

(1) a. … he had nearly persuaded the young lady to go up and ask him   (1950, FIC)
his name.
b. … lawyers dissuaded the mother from filing suit.   (1951, MAG)
c. Perhaps I can persuade her into paying you …   (1875, FIC)

The sentences in (1a–c) illustrate different syntactic constructions in English, but they are similar in that all of them exhibit object control. In each sentence the higher verb—*persuade* in (1a, c) and *dissuade* in (1b)—selects three arguments, assigning them semantic roles. The first argument is the subject of the higher clause, which has the role of Agent in each case. The second is the direct object of the higher clause, which bears the Patient or Undergoer role. It is worth noting that in each case the argument status of the post-verbal NP means that the sentences are control constructions, and that they are not NP Movement structures.

As far as the third argument is concerned, its syntactic form varies in the three sentences. In (1a) it is a *to* infinitival clause, in (1b) it is what may be termed a *from -ing* complement, and in (1c) it may be termed an *into -ing* complement. The sentences in (1a–c) show that object control constructions may involve both *to* infinitives and *-ing* clauses, which may also be termed gerunds. In each of (1a–c) it may be assumed that the complement is sentential, because this assumption makes it possible to represent the argument structure of the lower verb and the semantic roles assigned by the lower verb in an economical fashion. The understood subject of a sentential complement in a control structure is represented with the label PRO, as is normal in the literature today. The label Goal may be assigned to the third argument of the object control structures in question.

A more specific set of semantic labels for the three arguments was proposed by Sag and Pollard (1991). They write:

> Verbs of the *order/permit* type all submit to a semantic analysis involving STATES OF AFFAIRS (SOAS) where a certain participant (the referent of the object) is influenced by another participant (the referent of the subject) to perform an action (characterized in terms of the soa denoted by the VP complement). The influencing participant may be an agent (as in *Kim persuaded Sandy to*

leave) or a nonagent (as in *Ignorance of thermodynamics compelled Pat to enroll in a poetry class*). The semantics of all verbs in this class thus involves a soa whose relation is of the INFLUENCE type. With respect to such soas, we may identify three semantic roles, which we will refer to as INFLUENCE (the possibly agentive influencer), INFLUENCED (the typically animate participant influenced by the influence) and SOA-ARG (the action that the influenced participant is influenced to perform) (or, in the case of verbs like *prevent* and *forbid*, NOT to perform). [Note omitted] (Sag and Pollard 1991, 66)

The terms and the analysis proposed by Sag and Pollard are well suited to the examples of object control given in (1a–c), but the more traditional set of labels is retained here, in line with most of the literature on object control.

This study examines some aspects of an important generalization relating to object control that has been proposed in the literature. This is Bach's Generalization. It is formulated most succinctly by Rizzi in (2):

(2)   In object control structures the object NP must be structurally   (Rizzi 1986,
       represented.   503)

Bach's Generalization is supported for instance by the data in (3a–d), from Rizzi (1986, 503):

(3)   a.   This leads people to the following conclusion.
       b.   This leads to the following conclusion.
       c.   This leads people [PRO to conclude what follows].
       d.   *This leads [PRO to conclude what follows].

The pattern of (3c), of the same type as (1a), is one of object control. Bach's Generalization then explains why the direct object of the matrix sentence, which is the controller of PRO, cannot be omitted in (3c). These sentences may in turn be compared with (3a) and (3b): Bach's Generalization only applies in object control, and therefore it does not disallow (3b), with the direct object omitted, since the latter does not involve control.

Some scholars have questioned the status of Bach's Generalization, but the present authors regard it as useful in the study of object control constructions and in drawing attention to the retention or omission of direct objects in such constructions. At the same time, the generalization is not a linguistic universal, and even in English there are exceptions to it. It is the purpose of the present chapter to investigate a class of such potential exceptions.[1] The class of exceptions in question concerns the verb *warn*, as in (4):

(4) The Humane Society of New York wishes to warn against   (1993, COHA, NEWS)
     trapping dogs and cats.

The third argument of sentence (4) may be termed an *against -ing* complement. It is a gerund introduced by the preposition *against*, and consisting of a preposition and a gerund, it is similar to the *from -ing* and *into -ing* complements of (1b) and (1c) above. It also seems clear that the *against -ing* clause has an understood subject in (4), as in the other prepositional gerunds. It may be noted that the verb *warn* readily accepts a direct object that could act as the controller of PRO in (4), and a general NP such as *people* suggests itself in the case of (4):

(5) The Humane Society of New York wishes to warn people against trapping dogs and cats.

However, because sentence (4) is well formed, we are dealing with an exception to Bach's Generalization, provided that the Generalization is understood to mean that in object control constructions the controller of PRO needs to be overtly represented. The pattern of (4) with the covert controller of PRO is here termed the covert object control construction. The purpose of the present chapter is to investigate the occurrence and the nature of this type of construction with the help of the Corpus of Historical American English, COHA, in American English in the last two centuries, and the study of COHA is supplemented with a consideration of the construction in selected decades of the Hansard Corpus. Both corpora are very large and well suited to serve as sources of data for this study. The study focuses on the verb *warn* as the matrix verb. The verb is fairly frequent in English, which makes it possible to focus on a specific construction selected by it.

5.2   Covert Object Control with *Warn* in COHA and Hansard

The search string first considered for retrieving data in this study was "[warn].[v*] against [v?g*]." However, this search string is less than satisfactory for the present purpose because of the possibility of insertions. For instance, consider sentence (6), which is taken from COHA:

(6) The author agrees, however, with Portis that "one can not warn too   (1946, NF)
emphatically against making the psychotherapeutic approach a new
panacea for all patients."

Insertions between *warn* and *against* are probably fairly rare, because of
the complement status of the constituent beginning with the preposition,
but they are not impossible, as is shown by (6), and in the interest of recall,
provision should be made for such insertions. Further, it is conceivable
that there might be insertions between *against* and the *-ing* clause; for
instance, it would be conceivable to find a word such as *ever* in that position. Therefore it seems necessary to adopt "[warn].[v*]" with the word
against within nine words to the right as the primary search string.[2] On
the advice of an anonymous reader, a secondary search string of the form
"warn* against *ing" was used in order to guard against errors in tagging.
These search strings are not ideal from the point of view of precision, but
are necessary for the sake of recall.[3]

The search string retrieves many irrelevant tokens. These are of different types. The search string does not refer to an *-ing* clause, and there are
some tokens retrieved where the constituent that follows the preposition
is non-sentential, as in (7a–c):

(7) a. Flood tide analyzes the present-day tax situation, warns against   (1938, MAG)
rising costs of government.
b. On the same day that Mr. Cole spoke, Senator Symington again   (1953, NEWS)
warned against thinking "which starts with a dollar ceiling ..."
c. It can work for a while, but Orser warns against it for the long   (2009, MAG)
term, ...

The search string also retrieves numerous tokens where the constituent
that follows the preposition is sentential, but where the construction
involves overt object control, as in (8a–c):

(8) a. I would warn her against paying exorbitant prices for books and   (1922, FIC)
objects of art.
b. I have told you this story, that you may be warned against   (1835, FIC)
indulging the rancor of party feelings.
c. Bingley must be warned against showing any particular attention   (2006, FIC)
in that direction.

(8b–c) illustrate sentences where the matrix clause of the verb *warn* is in the passive. In this type of structure the derived subject represents the direct object of the corresponding active version, and acts as the controller of the lower subject, as frequently happens in object control constructions. While overt object control constructions are not the focus of this investigation, it is of interest to compare their frequency with *warn* to the frequency of covert object control constructions, and this consideration also supports the search string chosen.

Here are three initial examples of sentences that are relevant here. Sentence (9a) is the earliest example of the construction in the corpus, (9b) is from the early twentieth century, and (9c) is from current American English:

(9) a. … I believe the cause of poverty will often be found to exist in   (1829, FIC)
         the destitution of that economy, which warns against spending
         the little "all for that which is not bread, and the labour for that
         which satisfieth not."

     b. I mention them here only for the sake of completeness and in   (1901, NF)
         order to warn against attaching undue importance to them so far
         as the Pueblos …

     c. … they warn against drawing quick conclusions based solely on   (2000, MAG)
         the number of …

Examining the incidence of tokens systematically, the first conclusion to draw concerns the distribution of the construction in the course of the last two centuries. Table 5.1 gives information on the frequency of the construction in the decades covered by the corpus, with the size referring to millions of words and with normalized frequencies per million words given in parentheses.

Figure 5.1 below gives a linear representation of the progress of the overt and covert tokens over the course of the last two centuries.

The data in Table 5.1 and Fig. 5.1 show that in the first two decades of the corpus, both the overt and covert control constructions with *warn* were very rare. From the 1830s and particularly the 1840s onwards, the overt control construction started becoming more frequent, with the frequency getting closer to one per million in the 1840s. In later decades their frequencies are close to one per million for many decades, but only rarely do they go over one. It is also observed that there is considerable fluctuation in the frequency of the overt object control construction. As

Table 5.1   The incidence of overt and covert object control in the decades of COHA

Decade	Size	Overt tokens	Covert tokens
1810s	1.2	1 (0.8)	0
1820s	6.9	3 (0.4)	1 (0.1)
1830s	13.8	6 (0.4)	1 (0.1)
1840s	16.0	12 (0.8)	0
1850s	16.5	16 (1)	1 (0.1)
1860s	17.1	13 (0.8)	0
1870s	18.6	13 (0.7)	0
1880s	20.3	19 (0.9)	1 (0.0)
1890s	20.6	14 (0.7)	0
1900s	22.1	23 (1)	2 (0.1)
1910s	22.7	12 (0.5)	2 (0.1)
1920s	25.7	28 (1.1)	2 (0.1)
1930s	24.6	25 (1)	6 (0.2)
1940s	24.3	19 (0.8)	7 (0.3)
1950s	24.5	14 (0.6)	17 (0.7)
1960s	24.0	23 (1)	11 (0.5)
1970s	23.8	21 (0.9)	11 (0.5)
1980s	25.3	19 (0.8)	12 (0.5)
1990s	27.9	15 (0.5)	18 (0.6)
2000s	29.6	13 (0.4)	20 (0.7)

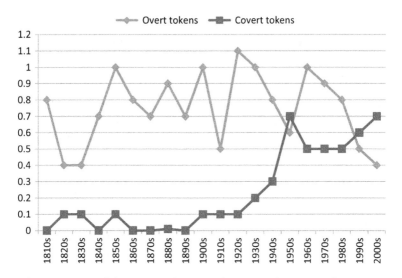

Fig. 5.1   Progress of the overt and covert tokens over the course of two centuries in COHA

far as the twentieth century is concerned, the frequency fluctuates noticeably up until the 1960s, and after that the corpus data indicates a gradual
decline.

As far as the covert object control construction is concerned, its frequency remained extremely low for the entire nineteenth century. In the
first three decades of the twentieth century the frequency remained low,
but two tokens were found in each of these decades. From the 1930s
onwards the frequency of the construction begins to rise in a noticeable
fashion. A peak of sorts occurs in the 1950s when the frequency reaches
that of the overt object control construction. In the next three decades it
falls behind again, but the construction does not fall into disuse. In the
two most recent decades, its frequency rises, with the most recent decade
being noteworthy in that its frequency is clearly higher than that of the
overt control construction. Overall, there is a relatively constant increase
of the covert object control construction during the latter half of the
twentieth century.

The increasing availability of covert object control with *warn* may be
linked to a general increase of *-ing* complements as reported in e.g.
Fanego (1996a, 1996b), Duffley (2000), Rudanko (2000, 2002) and
Vosberg (2006, 2009), and to one aspect of the Great Complement
Shift. As Rohdenburg (2006, 143–144) has observed, an important
aspect of this process concerns the spread of *-ing* complements of various types in recent centuries, and the emergence of the covert object
control pattern with *warn* involving the preposition *against* with a following *-ing* form suggests itself as one type of construction that fits well
into the general trend favoring the rise and spread of *-ing* complements
in recent times.

There is another, more specific consideration that may also have pro-
moted the emergence of the covert object control construction with *warn*.
As was noted above, the verb also selects non-sentential complements of
the type of (10).

(10) An editorial in the first issue of Free World warns against the   (1941, MAG)
      delusion of an easy victory.

While the non-sentential pattern of the type of (10) is not the main
focus of this investigation, it also involves a covert object, and the present
authors also investigated the frequency of the pattern of (10) in the first

six decades of the twentieth century. This period was chosen because it was during this time that the covert object control pattern was emerging. The study was then also extended to the nineteenth century to shed light on the status of Bach's Generalization during that century, given the finding above that implicit controllers were very rare during that century. The results are given in Table 5.2.

With respect to the nineteenth century Table 5.2 shows that implicit direct objects were rare in non-control *against* NP constructions with *warn* during that century. While overall numbers are low, the table also shows that such complements were more frequent than implicit controllers in the object control pattern, detailed in Table 5.1.

Table 5.2 reveals further that the frequency of the covert non-sentential patterns had a clearly rising trend from 1900 onwards, during the period when the covert object control pattern was emerging. Furthermore, it appears that the frequency of the non-sentential pattern showed a rising tendency that slightly preceded the rise of the covert gerundial construction. This suggests that the spread of the non-sentential pattern may have played a part in promoting the rise of the covert gerundial pattern.

Returning to sentential complements of *warn* with covert object control, it may be seen that there are 20 relevant tokens in the data in the 2000s.

Table 5.2 The frequency of the covert *against* NP construction with *warn* from 1810 to 1959

Decade	Number of tokens	Frequency
1810s	0	0.00
1820s	1	0.14
1830s	1	0.07
1840s	1	0.06
1850s	1	0.06
1860s	4	0.23
1870s	4	0.22
1880s	1	0.05
1890s	0	0.00
1900s	3	0.14
1910s	12	0.53
1920s	19	0.74
1930s	31	1.26
1940s	35	1.44
1950s	44	1.80

Further, the investigator cannot help noticing that many of them—nine in all—are from sociopolitical texts and discourses. Here are two illustrations:

(11) a. Former U.S. Ambassador to Saudi Arabia Wyche Fowler warns   (2001, MAG)
        against assuming that "monarchs can do anything they want
        without consequences ..."
     b. In the speech, focused on Iraq, Mr. McCain will warn against   (2007, NEWS)
        making policy on the war based on "the temporary favor of
        the latest ..."

Example (11a) is from *TIME* magazine, and there are two other tokens from the same magazine among the nine tokens from the sociopolitical field. As for tokens involving overt object control in this field in this decade, there are only three of them, which suggests that the covert object control construction may be especially popular in this area of language use.

Turning to British English, it should be noted that at the present time there is as yet no large corpus of diachronic British English that would fully match the scope of COHA as regards its balance of different text types. The Hansard Corpus is restricted to one text type, political speech, but it is diachronic and large enough in size to shed at least some light on possible violations of Bach's Generalization in fairly recent British English. Another reason for considering data from Hansard in this connection is because it was observed above that such violations may be likely to occur in political speech. The Hansard corpus is very large at 1.6 billion words, and for practical reasons, every third decade was selected for consideration, beginning with the 1820s. However, in view of the findings for American English reported above, which showed a spectacular increase in the frequency of the covert patterns in recent English, it was decided to include all decades from the 1910s onwards within the scope of the study. The search strings used were the same as for American English.

Table 5.3 gives information on the incidence of the overt and covert object control patterns with the verb *warn* in the decades examined, with the normalized frequencies given in parentheses.[4]

Figure 5.2 below gives a linear representation of the incidence of the two types of constructions in the decades examined.

Two illustrations of each type from the Hansard Corpus are given in (12a–b) and (13a–b).

Table 5.3 The incidence of the overt and covert object control patterns in selected decades of the Hansard Corpus

Decade	Size	Overt tokens	Covert tokens
1820s	11.6	18 (1.6)	0
1850s	33.0	84 (2.5)	0
1880s	60.0	91 (1.5)	0
1910s	79.8	53 (0.7)	0
1920s	71.7	41 (0.6)	0
1930s	95.2	49 (0.5)	1 (0.0)
1940s	94.8	39 (0.4)	1 (0.0)
1950s	121.0	51 (0.4)	1 (0.0)
1960s	152.0	55 (0.4)	9 (0.1)
1970s	163.3	50 (0.3)	7 (0.0)
1980s	183.7	54 (0.3)	24 (0.1)
1990s	177.1	53 (0.3)	22 (0.1)
2000s	88.4	17 (0.2)	14 (0.2)

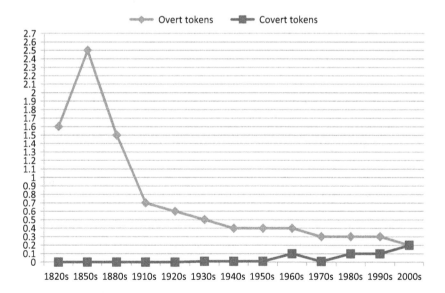

Fig. 5.2 Progress of the overt and covert tokens in selected decades of the Hansard Corpus

(12) a. I would earnestly warn the Government against trying to overdo   (1947)
     things: ...
   b. Fischer, the German Foreign Minister, warned smaller countries—and I (2003)
     repeat "warned"—against questioning the draft constitution.
(13) a. ... anxious, of course, to present a good balance sheet every month, to (1949)
     warn against giving drawing rights and credits, and even making
     outright gifts: ...
   b. ... in opening the debate the Home Secretary may have been wise to   (2000)
     warn against overstating one's case, ...

When comparing the results on British English based on the Hansard corpus with those on American English based on COHA, the investigator should not lose sight of the difference in respect of text type between the two corpora. However, similarly to the American English corpus, the British English corpus shows that in the selected decades of the nineteenth century the overt object control pattern occurred with a fair frequency, of about 1.8 per million words, whereas the covert object control pattern was almost non-existent in that century. In the twentieth century the overt pattern continued to be considerably more frequent than the covert pattern for several decades, but from the 1960s and the 1970s onwards the covert pattern began to be found in more noticeable numbers. Even in the most recent decade of the corpus, the 2000s, represented by the years from 2000 to 2005, the overt pattern is more frequent in Hansard, but the covert pattern is not very far behind in this period. There is thus a generally rising trend in the proportion of covert tokens in British English over the last 50 years or so. It is recalled that a rising trend was also observed in American English above, but it is also possible to say, subject to modification in light of later work, that the data from COHA suggest that the rising trend may have started slightly earlier in American English, especially with respect to the 1930s, 1940s and 1950s.

5.3   ANALYZING THE COVERT OBJECT CONTROL PATTERN SELECTED BY *WARN*

Turning to the interpretation of constructions with covert controllers, it is helpful to refer to the discussion of unexpressed objects in Huddleston and Pullum (2002). One of their classes in their discussion of what they call "transitive/intransitive contrasts" has the heading "Unexpressed human object," and it is directly relevant because the verb *warn* is listed in that class.[5] They write:

> We interpret the intransitives as having a human object, but it may be either general (arbitrary people), as in *That dog bites*, or specific, e.g. *you* in particular, as in a salient interpretation of *Take care: it may bite*. (Huddleston and Pullum 2002, 303)

The distinction between general and specific understood objects is of direct relevance to the class of *warn* in Huddleston and Pullum (2002, 303), but the application of these notions to actual data is not always easy, and there are gray areas between prototypical examples, as in the invented tokens in Huddleston and Pullum, and less clear cases. As regards the interpretation of covert objects, Rizzi (1986) gives considerable prominence to objects that are arbitrary or general. One of his examples is *Yesterday John warned (everyone) against this mistake*. He analyzes the covert object version of this sentence with the help of the label *arb*, defined as "a cover term for the feature specification identifying the set of properties generally referred to as 'arbitrary interpretation': [+human, +generic, +/−plural]" (Rizzi 1986, 509). With respect to the present data, the number of covert tokens in COHA in the nineteenth century and the first three decades of the twentieth is low, only ten. Caution needs to be exercised in drawing conclusions about the nature of the covert object on the basis of a small number of tokens, but it seems that in these early examples the covert object tends to be interpreted in a general way. Two illustrations from among the eight tokens are given in (14a–b):

(14) a. It [the Assembly of the Presbyterian Church] warns against "unduly extending the plea of necessity,"—against making it a cover for the love and practice of slavery. (1856, FIC)

b. While the sages warned against pampering the flesh, exalting the soul and mind, and deeming the body merely a corrupt thing, at best ... (1917, MAG)

From the 1930s onwards, numbers of tokens of the covert control construction begin to go up in COHA, and covert objects with less general interpretations also begin to become more prominent.[6] Only very rarely are the interpretations as specific as in the Huddleston and Pullum example *Take care: it may bite*, where the covert object was interpreted as *you*, but consider the sentences in (15a–c) from the 1930s and 1940s:

(15) a. The Board was to create NRA policy in the broadest terms, but the   (1935,
       memorandum warned against ever permitting the Board to attempt   MAG)
       executive functions, which were to be left to some efficient
       administrator to replace myself.

   b. Gen. R. E. Wood, president of Sears Roebuck and Co., another   (1937,
      witness, warned against drafting the bill in such a way as to centralize   NEWS)
      factories in cities or to "freeze" existing current conditions.

   c. He pleaded with Congress to reject the bill, warned against   (1943,
      quarreling "among ourselves in a vain effort to better or even hold   NEWS)
      our position at the expense of the other fellow," ...

The clue to interpreting the covert object is naturally found in the nature of the lower clause and its predicate. For instance, in (15a) the reference is restricted to those privy to the memorandum, and those who exercise authority over the Board. At the same time there is some indeterminacy because the individuals are not precisely specified. In (15b) the predicate *draft the bill* presumably restricts the reference of PRO and of the covert object primarily to Congressmen. As far as (15c) is concerned, the reflexive *ourselves* in the lower clause is worth noting. Since the reflexive needs to be bound, it follows that PRO and the covert direct object are likewise interpreted as referring to the same individuals. In a sense this is a very specific interpretation, since we are dealing with one particular NP in the language, but at the same time it may be added that in the example the pronoun in question for its part may well be interpreted in an inclusive way, again involving indeterminacy.

The low numbers of tokens up to the 1930s make it difficult to make definitive statements about long-term trends, but the data that are available suggest that the increasing frequency of the construction may have coincided with an increase in the potentially less general interpretation of covert objects. To gain a view of the current state of affairs, the data from the 2000s in COHA and Hansard were examined more closely. Consider the examples in (16a–b), (17a–b) and (18) in COHA.

(16) a.   What does the Bible mean when it warns against "sparing the rod"?   (2001,
                                                                               MAG)

   b.   Telephoto surveillance cameras peer down, armed police patrol the   (2001,
          border, bright yellow signs warn against taking any photographs or   NF)
          making so much as a note or a simple sketch, under the penalties
          of the Internal Security Act.

(17) a. Times editorials insisted the danger from Iraq was imminent. (2005,
When the Clinton administration attempted to negotiate, they NEWS)
warned against letting "diplomacy drift into dangerous delay. Even
a few more weeks free of inspections might allow Mr. Hussein to
revive construction of a biological, chemical or nuclear weapon."

   b. In the speech, focused on Iraq, Mr. McCain will warn against (2007,
making policy about the war based on "the temporary favor of the MAG)
latest public opinion poll" and assert that the administration's
strategy for securing Baghdad is the right one, according to
excerpts released Tuesday by his campaign. The other two leading
presidential contenders are Rudolph W. Guiliani of New York and
Mitt Romney of Massachusetts.

(18) Yes, he'd be the one to catch this cat. He'd kill it. He'd prove himself. (2008,
What had his brother said? He'd warned against pulling the snare too FIC)
early. If the cat was startled all would be lost.

In (16a) the covert object does not refer to a totally arbitrary set of people; instead, the reference is primarily to parents, but this still seems general, and in (16b) the co-text, including the use of *any* with the plural in the NP *photographs* suggests an even more general interpretation. On the other hand, (18) is rather exceptional in that the reference appears to be to one specific person, to the referent of the NP *his*, and seems about as specific as in the *Take care: it may bite* example from Huddleston and Pullum. Examples of this type are rare, but they are of interest in the context of the prominence assigned to general or arbitrary controllers in Rizzi's (1986) approach.

Between the examples in (16a–b) and (18) there are tokens of the type illustrated in (17a–b). In sentence (17a) the reference of the understood object may be to the Clinton administration, but it also presumably encompasses members of Congress, whose support for an attack on Iraq would be desirable or even necessary, and beyond that it presumably also extends to political opinion makers, including editorial writers of newspapers and columnists, whose support would also be important for such an attack to succeed. The extract in (17b) relates to the 2007 Republican primary campaign and McCain's warning may be directed at his Republican opponents, named in the extract, but it again extends beyond that to opinion makers and probably also to potential voters in Republican primaries. McCain could have spelled out his target with an overt NP, but the use of the covert construction creates an indeterminacy that can be a more effective means of persuasion than a more direct rhetorical technique. Some indeterminacy or fuzziness in the reference of the covert object seems common among the 20 tokens in the data from the 2000s in COHA.

With respect to the 13 tokens in Hansard from the 2000s, there are one or two tokens where a general interpretation is possible, as in (19a), but very specific interpretations are hard to find and in most tokens the understood object appears to have some indeterminacy in its reference, as in (19b).

(19) a. The report to which the noble Lord, Lord Northbourne, referred,   (2003)
          from the Royal College of Paediatrics and Child Health, rightly warns
          against assuming that professionals will always know best without
          listening seriously to parents: Parents need to feel respected and
          valued:

      b. ...I questioned the wisdom of allowing a general right to roam over   (2000)
          extensively grazed land because that is the very environment that is
          under the greatest ecological threat: Typically, the areas that we are
          referring to are moorland, heath and heather uplands: They are
          delicately balanced areas, and I warned against putting them under
          ever-greater pressure with the inevitable further decline in upland
          ground-laying species of birds:

In example (19b) the speaker is arguing against a "general right to roam." The understood controller of PRO may refer to some set of Members of Parliament and to interest groups lobbying Parliament for legislation, but the actual threat to land might come from those who would actually be roaming on the land in question, which again illustrates a type of indeterminacy that would not arise if the NP in question were spelled out.

The very indeterminacy of the covert object control construction may also be a reason why the pattern has spread so rapidly. This spread should be seen in the broad context of the Great Complement Shift, for one central aspect of the Shift concerns the spread of -*ing* clauses. In view of the infrequency of the covert object control pattern in the nineteenth century, its growing frequency in recent decades in both American English and British English may be viewed as the adding of a new grammatical construction to the language. Given that a construction is expected to consist of a certain form and of a certain meaning, the indeterminacy of the new construction means that the new construction fills a niche in the system of English predicate complementation, and can be expected to spread further.

There is also a more specific aspect to the use of the covert object control construction. The indeterminacy of the construction gives the speaker more deniability and more "wiggle room" than the overt object construction, where the object is spelled out. In this respect the covert object construction may be compared with the vagueness of passives without expressed *by* phrases. To shed light on the comparison, it is worth quoting van Oosten on what she suggests is one of the reasons for using agentless passives:

> The speaker wishes to leave the identity of the agent vague, for such reasons as politeness or expediency, or, sometimes, to reduce the assertion of responsibility for the agent. (van Oosten 1984, 14; see also Brown and Levinson 1987, 273–274 and Wanner 2009, 193)

The speech act of warning—or, more specifically, that of warning against, in the present case—is face threatening, relating to negative face, because it is designed to reduce the freedom of the person who is being warned against some act or some course of action. Not spelling out the identity of the person or persons in question is one way of mitigating the face threat inherent in the speech act in question. Four examples are given in (20a–d), where mitigation of face threat may be a consideration for the use of the covert pattern.

(20) a. They are delicately balanced areas, and I warned against putting them under ever-greater pressure with the inevitable further decline in upland ground-laying species... (Hansard, 2000)

b. Mr Digby Jones, director general of the CBI, warned, as I have done, against compelling and, forcing good firms to defend themselves unnecessarily when their European rivals shelter under less rigorous regimes. (Hansard, 2002)

c. I return to the Secretary of State's speech, in which he warned against falling into the trap of considering the industry along outdated nationalistic lines, and observed that both Government and industry have a role in promoting the multinational reality of the defense industry today: (Hansard, 2003)

d. Former U.S Ambassador to Saudi Arabia Wyche Fowler warns against assuming that "monarchs can do anything they want without consequences from a restless or dissident citizenry." (COHA, 2001, MAG)

In (20a–c) the warnings are indirect, with the speaker reporting a warning issued earlier either by himself or herself or by somebody else, to the addressee or addressees in the context of the original communication, in order to bolster the case against a certain course of action in that context. Reported warnings can function as warnings, provided that the person or body whose warning is being reported is presented by the speaker or writer as authoritative or trustworthy and such indirect warnings appear to be fairly common in a political context in the present data. In (20d), with present tense *warns*, the situation is ongoing, and the warning seems more direct. In either case the utterance sounds less confrontational when the person or persons who are being warned against a certain course of action are not identified.

5.4   Concluding Observations

Bach's Generalization is an important condition making predictions about an aspect of the system of English predicate complementation, but it is not an absolute rule, and the present study explores a class of potential counterexamples to it. The construction considered is *warn against -ing*. A corpusbased study of the construction in American English is made possible by the availability of COHA, and the availability of the Hansard Corpus makes it possible to shed light on it in one text type of British English. Both corpora are large, making it possible to investigate even rare patterns. It is observed that the construction was very rare in the nineteenth century, but that it became considerably more frequent in the course of the twentieth century. The increase in frequency is manifested both in the overall frequency of the construction, and in the proportion of the covert object control construction with *warn* in relation to the overt object control construction with this verb. Thus it was observed that in the last two decades of COHA, the totals of the covert construction were higher than those of the overt construction. In the Hansard data the covert construction did not reach the frequency of the overt construction, but still showed a clear rise in the most recent decades.

The reasons for the increasing frequency of the covert object control construction will deserve further investigation. On the basis of the data considered here, it may be suggested that it is especially in political English that the construction is popular. Thus many of the more recent examples in COHA were from newspapers or magazines, especially from *TIME* magazine, and the content of the examples often reveals their origin in political English. The study also examined the interpretation of the covert object, suggesting that there may have been a tendency for early covert objects to have a general interpretation and for less general interpretations to have become more prominent in the course of time. However, very specific interpretations continue to be very rare, and often there is a degree of vagueness or indeterminacy in the interpretation of the covert object. This very indeterminacy may have fostered the spread of the construction in political English, for it gives a speaker an opportunity of issuing a warning while leaving the precise identity of the persons warned indeterminate. A reason for this may have to do with mitigating the face-threatening nature of a warning. This kind of indeterminacy may be especially attractive in political rhetoric, where a speaker may also want to leave himself or herself some "wiggle room" or scope for deniability in his or her statements.

In the light of the present study it will be of interest further to examine the role of text type in violations of Bach's Generalization. It will also be of interest to investigate whether other matrix verbs of object control may show changes in favor of detransitivization similar to those observed with *warn*, and if so, whether the interpretation of implicit objects in their case may be similar to what was observed in this study. A further extension will be to compare violations of Bach's Generalization and the incidence of implicit objects in contexts with no following sentential complement.

NOTES

1. Landau (2013, 178–179) is among the studies that question the status of Bach's Generalization. In support of her position, Landau notes that while the verbs *convince*, *persuade*, and *urge* do not permit the controller of PRO to be omitted—or to be implicit—in object control constructions, which is in accordance with Bach's Generalization, these verbs do not permit the direct object to be implicit in non-control constructions either, since for instance * *We urged to a moral life* is ill-formed, alongside of the well-formed *We urged him to a moral life*. She takes this to mean that the lack of omissibility of direct objects is a "lexical property of the verbs [...] independent of control" (2013, 178–179). An appeal to lexical properties is possible, but Bach's Generalization still seems useful for a number of reasons. First, it sheds light on the behavior of verbs of the type of *lead*, as was noted in the text. Second, while verbs such as *urge* subcategorize for sentential complements with object control and for relevant non-sentential complements of the type pointed out by Landau, with the direct object not omissible in either type, there are other verbs, including *teach* and *instruct*, which also subcategorize for sentential complements with object control, but do not easily permit relevant non-sentential complements. (It may be worth noting that the verb *teach* is used by Bresnan (1982, 418) to illustrate Bach's

Generalization.) For instance, while *Jonas had taught her to play chess...* (COCA, 2010, FIC) is good, a non-sentential complement of the type **Jonas had taught her to chess* is not. Nevertheless, the omission of the object is disallowed in the object control construction: **Jonas had taught to play chess*. This is explained by Bach's Generalization. More broadly, Bach's Generalization is useful because it privileges the task of comparing control and non-control constructions and their implicit objects and invites further work on the nature of such implicit objects.

2. The searches for COHA were conducted in May 2012. The limitation to nine words to the right arises because this is the maximum context range permitted in COHA.

3. While almost all the relevant tokens were retrieved using the primary search string, the secondary search string did uncover two additional tokens.

4. Again almost all tokens were retrieved using the primary search string, and the secondary search string retrieved only four additional tokens.

5. Under the same heading "Unexpressed human object" Huddleston and Pullum also refer to a class of verbs, including *please*, that "appear more readily in intransitives when the situation is habitual or unactualized," noting a contrast between *He never fails to please* and ?*His behavior at lunch pleased* (Huddleston and Pullum 2002, 303). *Warn* is not in the *please* class, and the focus here is on the nature of the understood object with *warn*, but a comment may be inserted on the concepts proposed for that class. A habitual situation may be seen as contrasting with a one-off situation or event and an unactualized event may be contrasted with an actualized situation or event. The actualized versus unactualized contrast and the role it may play in the case of *warn* may be related to a distinction under the label of "mode," as outlined in Hopper and Thompson (1980, 252) in their discussion of transitivity:

> Mode: This refers to the distinction between "realis" and "irrealis" encoding of events. An action which either did not occur, or which is presented as occurring in a non-real (contingent) world, is obviously less effective than one whose occurrence is actually asserted as corresponding directly with a real event.

The relevant sense of *warn* is "to give (a person) cautionary notice or advice with regard to actions or conduct; to caution against neglect of duty or against wrong or mistaken action or belief" (*OED*, *warn*, v.[1], sense 4.a; constructions with *against* under 4.b), and it follows from this meaning that the content of the lower clause may often be unactualized. However, in the construction with *warn* the omission of the object, while a feature of reduced transitivity, is in the higher clause, and for this reason it may be inappropriate to link it to the reduced transitivity of the lower clause.

As for the contrast between habitual and one-off situations or events, consider sentence (i).

(i) The Health Department sent out 0,000 [sic] placards   (COHA,
     yesterday warning against spitting, to be displayed in cars,   1920, NEWS)
     public buildings, and other places where all may read.

The warning in (i) should be understood as a warning not only against a habit of spitting but even against a single act of spitting. The *-ing* form has sometimes been associated—in other constructions in English grammar— with "regular activity" (Allerton 1988, 21), a term which seems akin to the notion of habitual action or activity, but sentence (i) shows that in the covert object control construction it also permits a one-off interpretation. Similar one-off interpretations often appear to be possible in other tokens of covert control, as in (11a–b) in the text.

6. The possibility of less general and more specific interpretations of covert objects in the covert control construction with *warn* was also illustrated in Rudanko (2001). One of the illustrations in that source is the following, from the *Washington Post*:

(i) They thought that they, rather than reform-minded   (*Washington Post*, April
     administrators, ought to be the judge of what best   3, 1994, cited in
     inspired their students. Many critics warn against   Rudanko 2001,
     adhering too closely to any formula.   137–138)

References

Allerton, David J. 1988. 'Infinitivitis' in English. In *Essays on the English Language and Applied Linguistics on the Occasion of Gerhard Nickel's 60th Birthday*, ed. Josef Klegraf and Dietrich Nehls, 11–23. Heidelberg: Groos.

Bresnan, Joan. 1982. Control and Complementation. *Linguistic Inquiry* 13 (3): 343–434.

Brown, Penelope, and Stephen C. Levinson. 1987. *Politeness: Some Universals in Language Use*. Cambridge: Cambridge University Press.

Duffley, Patrick J. 2000. Gerund versus Infinitive as Complement of Transitive Verbs in English: The Problems of 'Tense' and 'Control'. *Journal of English Linguistics* 28: 221–248.

Fanego, Teresa. 1996a. The Development of Gerunds as Objects of Subject-Control Verbs in English (1400–1760). *Diachronica* 13: 29–62.

————. 1996b. The Gerund in Early Modern English: Evidence from the Helsinki Corpus. *Folia Linguistica Historica* XVII: 97–152.

Hopper, Paul, and Sandra Thompson. 1980. Transitivity in Grammar and Discourse. *Language* 56 (2): 251–299.

Huddleston, Rodney, and Geoffrey Pullum. 2002. *The Cambridge Grammar of the English Language*. Cambridge: Cambridge University Press.

Landau, Idan. 2013. *Control in Generative Grammar: A Research Companion*. Cambridge: Cambridge University Press.

Oxford English Dictionary, 2nd ed. 1989. OED Online. Oxford: Oxford University Press. Accessed February 2017. http://www.oed.com

Rizzi, Luigi. 1986. Null Objects in Italian and the Theory of Pro. *Linguistic Inquiry* 17 (3): 501–557.

Rohdenburg, Günter. 2006. The Role of Functional Constraints in the Evolution of the English Complementation System. In *Syntax, Style and Grammatical Norms*, ed. Christiane Dalton-Puffer, Dieter Kastovsky, and Herbert Schendl, 143–166. Bern: Peter Lang.

Rudanko, Juhani. 2000. *Corpora and Complementation*. Lanham, MD: University Press of America.

————. 2001. *Case Studies in Linguistic Pragmatics*. Lanham, MD: University Press of America.

————. 2002. *Complements and Constructions*. Lanham, MD: University Press of America.

Sag, Ivan, and Carl Pollard. 1991. An Integrated Theory of Complement Control. *Language* 67: 63–113.

van Oosten, Jeanne. 1984. *The Nature of Subjects, Topics and Agents: A Cognitive Explanation*. UC Berkeley Dissertation, Berkeley, CA.

Vosberg, Uwe. 2006. *Die grosse Komplementverschiebung*. Tübingen, Germany: Narr.

————. 2009. Non-finite Complements. In *One Language, Two Grammars?* ed. Günter Rohdenburg and Julia Schlüter, 212–227. Cambridge: Cambridge University Press.

Wanner, Anja. 2009. *Deconstructing the English Passive*. Berlin: Mouton de Gruyter.

CHAPTER 6

Concluding Observations

Abstract This chapter reviews and compares the main findings of the four case studies presented in this book, and provides comment on the issues that have arisen during the course of the four studies. In the case of the three chapters on subject control in adjectival complement structures, the Choice Principle was shown to have a statistically significant effect in all cases, and it was noted that the progress of the gerundial complement option is more advanced with the lesser-used adjective *terrified* than it is with the higher-frequency adjectives *scared* and *afraid*. Chapter 5, dealing with object control with the verb *warn* and apparent violations of Bach's Generalization, presented evidence of the increasing frequency of the covert object pattern in British and American English, as well as arguments for the reasons behind the rise of these structures.

Keywords Choice Principle • Bach's Generalization • Adjectival complementation

The four case studies presented in Chaps. 2, 3, 4 and 5 of this book are all connected by the common thread of control. Subject control structures with three semantically related adjectives as matrix predicates are followed up by a case study dealing with object control in the context of the verbal predicate *warn*. In each chapter, evidence is drawn from large corpora of

© The Author(s) 2018
P. Rickman, J. Rudanko, *Corpus-Based Studies on Non-Finite Complements in Recent English*,
https://doi.org/10.1007/978-3-319-72989-3_6

recent British and American English. A diachronic perspective has been adopted in all studies, with the time-frame limited to the last two centuries of English. During this period there has been constructional competition between the *to* infinitive and the gerundial pattern in the adjectival predicate structures under examination in the present work, and it is during the same period that the development of the competing object control pattern of the verbal predicate *warn* has taken place. The decision to focus only on recent English can therefore be justified.

In the work on subject control, a major aim has been to contribute to what is already known about the ways in which the competing sentential complement patterns of adjectival predicates have been interacting in the recent history of English. The well-documented development and subsequent expansion of the gerund at the cost of other pre-existing patterns in recent centuries is a phenomenon encompassed by the Great Complement Shift, and it is against this general backdrop that the present work has been situated. The three adjectives chosen for study here all share the ability to license a *to* infinitive and a gerundial *of-ing* complement in present-day English. The adjectives in question are *scared, terrified* and *afraid*. The evidence provided in the present study has suggested that the effects of the Shift can be seen in varying degrees with each of the three adjectives, and that various factors may have contributed to the promotion or suppression of the gerund.

To assess the impact of various possible factors on the progress of the two complement types, two main principles were applied to the data; the well-established Extraction Principle was first tested as a possible syntactic factor that may have provided some support for the *to* infinitive to maintain its position. It was found in all relevant cases, however, that there were very few instances of extraction environments among the often high numbers of relevant tokens—a finding which was in itself noteworthy. The focus thus turned to semantic factors. The connection between the semantics of infinitival and gerundial competitors and complement selection has been widely discussed for decades, but a specific focus on the degree of agentivity seen in the lower clause subject and a possible connection to each complement type has not yet received widespread attention. Establishing a clear distinction between pairs such as *I was scared to go home* and *I was scared of going home* is not an easy task, but the recently proposed Choice Principle provides the lens through which the issue can be viewed. Building on the positive results of earlier studies of this type, statistical significance is derived from the application of the Choice

Principle in Chaps. 2, 3, and 4, and the overall results are encouraging. It is the hope of the present authors that the additional angle provided by the principle will be of benefit to future research in this area.

Chapter 2 led the investigation into adjectival complement selection, with the adjective *scared*. The chapter tracked the development of the *to* infinitive and the *of -ing* complements in the period covered by COHA. Although the *to* infinitive was a possible complement of *scared* as early as the 1820s, it was noted that such tokens were relatively scarce right up until the early 1900s. After this point the *of -ing* complement began to surface in the corpus data, and the frequency of both types began to increase, the *to* infinitive notably more so than the gerund. The study thus focused on the period from the 1910s onwards, this being the main period of any real type of variation between the two patterns. A large number of indirect *to* infinitive complements, as in *He was too scared to walk home alone*, were noted and duly set aside, as were the small number of tokens featuring extraction contexts following the application of the Extraction Principle. As predicted by the principle, all extractions were out of *to* infinitival complements. The application of the Choice Principle to the COHA data returned highly significant results in a Chi Square test, and it was noted that the *to* infinitive [+Choice] lower predicate was the most common type of the four possibilities. It was suggested that the relatively high number of *to* infinitives in the present-day dataset may be linked to the use of the negated form of this matrix predicate in stance-like interpretations.

The study then applied the same analyses to data from the BNC. The Choice Principle was found to have a highly significant effect also with this dataset, with *to* infinitive [+Choice] lower clause environments dominating. A comparison between the BNC results and those of the 1970s, 1980s and 1990s decades of COHA suggested that the gerundial complement was at a more advanced stage with *scared* in late twentieth century British English than it was in American English. These admittedly tentative findings invite further research in order to reveal more about the effects of the Great Complement Shift with this particular adjective among World Englishes.

Chapter 3 turned the attention to the adjective *terrified*, and employed the same corpora and applied the same methods as were introduced in Chap. 2. It was noted in the case of *scared* that according to the COHA data, the nineteenth century was not a period in which either sentential complement was commonly used with *scared*, and this pattern of usage was also apparent with *terrified*. In fact, parallel to the situation with *scared*, *terrified* was found with a mere handful of tokens of the *to* infinitive type from the early to mid-1800s onwards, and it was not until the early 1900s that the gerund began to appear alongside it. Frequencies for both infinitive and gerund remained modest throughout the twentieth century however, and the present-day distributions of the sentential complements of *terrified*—possibly as a result of the lower overall frequencies—are rather different. The gerund overtakes the infinitival complement as the twentieth century closes, and with the help of COCA data from the period 2000–2015, it was confirmed that the gerund is now the more frequent of the two complement types in American English. It was noted that negation with *terrified* is not common, compared to *scared*, and this in turn may have some bearing on the low numbers of *to* infinitives and the dominance of the gerund. It was also seen that the Extraction Principle was of limited applicability in the case of this adjective, with no cases of extraction found among the COHA data, and three among the COCA data.

The Choice Principle was applied to the decades of COHA from the 1950s onwards, and the results proved statistically significant in a Chi Square test. The COCA data was similarly examined for [+/−Choice] lower clause contexts, and this present-day dataset helped to demonstrate convincingly that the principle has a significant effect on complement selection. It was observed that the *of*-*ing* complement with a [−Choice] context is the most common combination. BNC data was added to the American English evidence, to reveal that the gerund is also the more common of the two sentential types in British English, and the Choice Principle also has relevance in this case.

Chapter 4 presented the last of the adjectival *fear* predicates, with an analysis of *afraid*. This appears to be overall the more frequent of the three adjectives in the present work, and in order to keep numbers manageable, only the decades of the 1820s, 1910s and 2000s were used from COHA. All data found in the BNC were used. The COHA data indicated that both complements were in use with *afraid* as early as the 1820s, with the *to* infinitive the more frequent but the gerund nevertheless present with a considerable frequency. Although both complements changed in frequency over the 180 years of American English covered by this study, the gerund has not been able to make a great deal of headway against the dominance of the infinitival complement. Cases of extraction were found in all decades of COHA used, but numbers were low when viewed in the light of the high overall frequencies. Results of the application of the Choice Principle echoed those of *scared* and *afraid*, with high levels of statistical significance in all cases. The BNC data showed a similar type of distribution and significance in relation to the Choice Principle.

In all three adjectival predicate structures, the connection between the inherently non-agentive nature of passive lower clauses and the gerundial complement was highlighted. Supplementary searches showed conclusively that *of -ing* complements are the more likely of the two sentential types to be found in passive lower clauses, as predicted by the Choice Principle.

The present series of studies into adjectival complementation has attempted to tackle several important questions, as well as open up opportunities for future research. It has been shown that the Choice Principle constitutes a valid addition to the theoretical toolbox available to researchers of complementation. While it was emphasized that it is unable to predict complement selection in a categorical way, the present studies have demonstrated that the principle can produce highly significant results. It was noted that dichotomies set up in earlier work to explain the contrasts between the *to* infinitive and the gerund when in variation are valuable, but not always applicable to all cases, the subject control scenario being one such case. The Choice Principle is thus best seen as a supplement to the literature already available, and not as a replacement. Further work is naturally desirable to examine the relation of the Choice Principle to factors identified in preexisting frameworks of analysis.

The notion of affective stance is a recurring theme throughout these three studies, and it was suggested that the semantic flexibility of the *to* infinitive that allows a stance-like interpretation is a factor that makes it easier for an adjectival predicate to continue to ward off the spread of the gerundial complement, ensuring an ongoing role for the *to* infinitive. It was noted that the stance-like usages of the adjectives *scared* and *afraid* were found with some frequency. *Terrified*, on the other hand, stood in sharp contrast to *scared* and *afraid* in this respect, as it was the one that does not seem to easily lend itself to the stance usage, and in addition it was the only one to show evidence of the gerund overrunning the territory of the infinitival complement.

The adjective *afraid* merits a further comment with respect to its infinitival and gerundial complements. On the basis of the study of three selected decades of COHA in Chap. 4, it appears that in the case of this adjective the relative proportions of *to* infinitive and *of -ing* complements have remained relatively stable in recent English. Stance-like interpretations of the *to* infinitive may have served to ward off the gerundial variant, but in addition, the high frequency of the infinitival construction with the adjective may also have protected its entrenched status. (The high frequency of the construction may also have fostered stance-like interpretations.) Further, as was noted, each type of construction was characterized by a high degree of semantic specialization with respect to the Choice Principle, which may also have served to protect the *to* infinitive from encroachment by the gerundial pattern.

Chapter 5 turned the focus from subject to object control, and from adjectival to verbal complementation. The guiding principle was Bach's Generalization, which states that direct objects in object control structures may not be omitted. Violations of the generalization are not unheard of, however, and data from recent decades of COHA were introduced to shed more light on direct object omission with *warn*, as seen in sentences such as *The committee warned against interfering in the election process.* This type of pattern, here termed the covert object pattern, was compared to the historically more dominant overt object pattern in COHA, and the data revealed a steady increase of the former at the expense of the latter over the twentieth century. Initial analysis pointed to the area of political discourse as a focal point of this change, with the suggestion that when the recipient of the warning is omitted, the warning becomes more diplomatic, less direct, and therefore useful from a pragmatic point of view. The spoken British English Hansard corpus data were then examined, and showed that the twentieth century rise of the covert object pattern was also evident here, but not to the same degree as that seen in COHA. According to the Hansard data, the covert had not yet overtaken the overt pattern in the area of British political discourse as of the mid 2000s—the two patterns instead exhibited roughly similar ratios.

A secondary aim of Chap. 5 was to offer comment on the relevance of Bach's Generalization, in the light of recent discussion regarding its importance in the literature. Weighing up the merits of the perspective that prioritizes the lexical properties of individual verbs versus the one that prefers to view such variation from the angle of linguistic generalizations (where possible), the present authors prefer not to underestimate the value of the latter view. Generalizations such as the one dealt with in Chap. 5, which allow exceptions and thus give rise to variation in language use, should be seen as valuable for their ability to facilitate discussion and investigation into the nature of the examples that run counter to the predictions they make. This, in turn, helps enrich our understanding of the larger mechanisms behind language usage, its variation and change.

The present book has focused on the nature and applicability of the Choice Principle and Bach's Generalization in the system of English predicate complementation. This study obviously invites follow-up work in a number of areas at the syntax-semantics interface: as far as the Choice Principle is concerned, the present investigation suggests that it is an explanatory factor bearing on the complement selection properties of the adjectives considered—*scared*, *terrified*, and *afraid*—but the present authors would not presume to claim that it can always be invoked, even partially, to explain variation between *to* infinitival and gerundial complements of matrix predicates that select both types of non-finite patterns. This points to the desirability of further work on other predicates, with the ultimate aim of finding a common denominator for the constructions to which the Choice Principle is salient.

As far as Bach's Generalization is concerned, it may be hoped that the present investigation represents a step forward in the analysis of the nature and use of the covert object construction selected by the matrix verb *warn*, and it invites further work on violations of Bach's Generalization in the case of other matrix predicates. In this connection it will be of interest to investigate whether the interpretation of the covert object put forward in the case of the matrix verb *warn* may be extended to other matrix predicates permitting violations of Bach's Generalization. Linked to the issue of the nature of the covert object is the question of whether the pragmatic explanation offered here for the use of the construction in political discourse may have relevance to violations of Bach's Generalization in the case of other matrix predicates. The present authors cherish the hope that other work will follow to explore such further questions in the analysis of the system of English predicate complementation.

Index[1]

---

[1] Note: Page numbers followed by 'n' refer to notes.

© The Author(s) 2018
P. Rickman, J. Rudanko, *Corpus-Based Studies
on Non-Finite Complements in Recent English*,
https://doi.org/10.1007/978-3-319-72989-3